Erasmus - Luther

DISCOURSE ON
FREE WILL

Translated and edited by

ERNST F. WINTER

CONTINUUM•NEW YORK

2000

The Continuum Publishing Company
370 Lexington Avenue
New York, NY 10017

Printed in the United States of America

Library of Congress Catalog Card No. 60-53363

ISBN 0-8044-6140-6

INTRODUCTION

LUTHER repeatedly described *The Enslaved Will* (*De servo arbitrio*, 1525) and his *Catechism* (1529) as the best expressions of his thought. He had been aroused to write this fierce tract because of Erasmus' *On Free Will* (*De libero arbitrio*, 1524). And Erasmus, though originally sympathetic to the reform movement within Christendom—he himself relates a popular expression, "Erasmus laid the egg which Luther hatched"—again attacked the Lutheran version of reform. Erasmus was afraid of religious disturbances. He was also prompted by friends, lay- and churchmen, to become partisan in the "great debate" of his time. Consequently, Erasmus and Luther argued over what they and their contemporaries thought was the characteristic difference between the evolving Catholic and Protestant positions concerning human nature, namely, the question of the freedom of the will. Their often heated discourse reveals, however, as much (if not more) about their subjective modes of thinking and about the atmosphere of this transition period from late Renaissance and Northern Humanism to Protestantism and post-Tridentine Catholicism, as about the perennial problem of man's free will. But in the history of ideas this discourse gains an added significance. It displays some of the possibilities and limitations of Christian Humanism. It sheds light on the subsequent development of modern thought. While the tools of both protagonists are often medieval, many of their insights and the issues themselves seem decidedly modern.

Well into the eighteenth century the Latin original of Erasmus was still being read. The Enlightenment had its picture of Erasmus, as did Romanticism and Liberalism in the nineteenth century. It is significant that the present Erasmus renaissance is revising all past pictures and, in particular, is attempting to show how orthodox, even Thomistic, Erasmus had been in his Christianity; that he is not just the "father of modernity" (cf. Bouyer and Mesnard), but more complex; that he has much to say on current problems. Equally significant is the reevaluation of Luther as a truly religious and committed man, who is not simply responsible for the modern age, but who also produced both conservative and liberal consequences to his thought.

The following introductory remarks introduce the reader to an obviously complex subject. A mere sketch of the life, works, temperament, and some views of both protagonists suffices to show how fascinatingly timely their topics have remained. The selected bibliography serves as a guide for further study.

Desiderius Erasmus was born in Rotterdam probably in 1466. He was the illegitimate son of a priest and a physician's daughter, a fact that depressed Erasmus all his life. Both parents died early. The boy who had never experienced family life craved for the rest of his days to be liked and appreciated. He was born into a time of turmoil and of partisanship. He obtained a good education at the famous school of the Brethren of the Common Life at Deventer (1474-1484). They instilled in him their pious "devotio moderna," a lay spirituality deeply affecting Northern Humanism. He became a monk and ordained priest at the Augustinian monastery at Steyn (1486-1493). His poor health and love for humanistic studies, plus dislike for the monks, gained him a temporary dispensation, which eventually Pope Leo X arranged in permanence. Leaving the monastery—as it turned out later—for good, he turned first to the University of Paris (1495). The budding humanist scholar was disappointed. Scholastic subtleties only increased the Humanists' antipathies to Aristotle, dialectic, and Scholasticism. Erasmus, too, protested against systematic philosophy. Instead, classical philology, a virgin field of endeavor, attracted him. To place it in the service of religion was a sentiment strengthened on repeated visits to

England, where he met devout Humanists like Colet and St. Thomas More. Study, writing, good companionship, and collecting valuables filled much of his life thereafter. He discovered and edited Lorenzo Valla's critical *Annotations* to the Vulgate (1505). His study of Greek and trips to Italy enriched his horizon. *In Praise of Folly* (1511) was a biting satire on human nature. The Church did not escape unscathed. The new Bible translation and critical edition of the Greek text, the *Novum Instrumentum* (1516), marked progress in higher textual criticism. And, although some great universities like Louvain, Oxford and Cambridge proscribed all his writings, many Renaissance churchmen actively sympathized with the "Erasmian reform" spirit.

The *95 Theses* a year thereafter (1517) ended this spirit's chances for success. A more radical approach to reform had commenced. Soon a much broader popular response than Erasmus ever had had for his wit was to accompany one Martin Luther. Fourteen years younger than Erasmus, he was born in Eisenach in 1483 to a mining family of peasant stock. In some respects he had strikingly similar experiences to Erasmus: studying at a Brethren school and imbibing the "devotio moderna"; experiencing the insecurity of home life and friction with his family; entering the Augustinian monastery of Erfurt (1505), after being nearly killed by lightning. Otherwise, however, profound differences existed. Erasmus had found inspiration in the Platonists, St. Jerome, Origen. Luther found his in St. Paul, St. Augustine. Erasmus, fond of humanistic studies, a comfortable life, correspondence with all the famed in the world, acquired increasingly growing popularity and domestic serenity. He became the acknowledged cosmopolitan head of the "respublica litteraria," writing in brilliant Latin. Luther's powerful German could not move Erasmus, who used to advantage the polished style of Renaissance tract literature, which, while pious, was quite witty. The *Adagia* (1500) are popularized Humanism. In short, Erasmus felt proud to be a "humanist genius."

Luther, on the other hand, felt happiest when seriously

concerned with the things of God. The Nominalist teaching of Gabriel Biel, a follower of William of Occam's philosophy, deepened Luther's problematic concern for the meaning of life, his own in particular. He could not find an answer in the classics, though he absorbed much learning. He turned increasingly to the consolation of faith. Still young, he was given the important chair of theology at Wittenberg (1512). When preparing his lectures, he turned completely from humanistic learning and Scholastic theology to a biblical exegesis of his own inspiration. In 1515 he found his desperate queries answered in the Epistle to the Romans (1, 17), in the concept of "justification by faith." Erasmus' *New Testament* helped him gain further insights.

Erasmus at first affirmed much in Luther, but increasingly objected to his "extremism and rough manners." The years 1517 and 1520 brought serious estrangements. The humanist followers of Luther wished Erasmus on their side, especially Melanchthon, who remained an ardent admirer of Erasmus all his life. But Luther's three fighting challenges to authority, as it existed in the Europe of his day, the *Address to the German Nobility, The Babylonian Captivity of the Church* and *The Liberty of a Christian,* brought the breach with Rome. In the same year a Roman bull, *Exsurge Domine* (1520), chastized Luther. He answered with the *Assertions,* which among other things, denied the free will. Erasmus hated to be drawn into this controversy and moved from Louvain to Basel (1521). The New Pope Adrian VI, a practical Netherlander, an old school friend of Erasmus, was genuinely interested in reform and wanted to see Erasmus do something, even come to Rome. Erasmus tried to shield his "neutrality" by suggesting both ill health and his favorite idea of a truce. A jury of independent scholars (including himself) ought to be able to settle the commotion with due reason. Luther, from the other side, sarcastically counseled Erasmus not to get involved and to disturb his love of peace. Erasmus replied to him that he greatly feared Satan's power might be deluding Luther. Finally, responding to both outward prodding and inner conviction ("At least *I* cannot be accused of abandoning the Gospel to the passions of men") Erasmus wrote in one sitting his *Diatribe seu collatio de libero arbitrio,* a classic treatise against Luther. It appeared September 1, 1524 in Basel.

The Pope, the Emperor, and Henry VIII (who himself had received the title "Defender of Faith" for writing against Luther (1521), congratulated Erasmus. The world considered the little book a beautifully written and ingenious tract. The issue was joined. Despite detractions by the "heavenly prophets," the outbreak of bloody peasant uprisings, and personal problems, Luther soon finished his four-times-longer answer, *De servo arbitrio* (December, 1525). The answer was as unsystematic as Erasmus' piece, but powerful in its conviction and denial of the freedom of the will. Erasmus was stung. His peace was gone. Luther must be answered. The resulting two lengthy volumes, *Hyperaspistes Diatribae adversus servum arbitrium M. Lutheri* (1526, 1527), are more careful than his earlier work. Luther is castigated as the destroyer of civil, religious, and cultural order and harmony. In a sense Erasmus offers a detailed explanation of Christian Humanism and humanistic theology, as he conceived both. But not even his conciliatory and pacific *On Restoring Concord in the Church* (1533), concluding with the admonition "tolerate each other," was able to bridge the enmity. His common sense and uncomplicated tolerance could not satisfy the committed seeker for truth. The conflict raged.

While this great duel did not resolve the thorny question of the freedom of the will, it did illustrate the basic views on the nature of man and God held by most contemporaries in the West at that time. These views reached into the past and were to rise to great importance with the coming of the national, industrial, democratic state. Their relevance today contribute to the Erasmian renaissance.

Luther's part in the debate is the emphasis on Christianity as dogmatic religion. He wants to solve the issue theologically. For Erasmus Christianity is morality, a simplicity of life and of doctrine. He wants to resolve the problem philosophically. In current terminology, Erasmus displays an anthropological concern, but employs essentially theological tools, without being or ever wanting to be a theologian. Luther fashions his own theological tools, without much interest in systematic structure. Erasmus has deep pastoral concern. Luther desires the truth to shine forth and the whole church to accept his witness to a personal commitment. He is therefore distressed by Erasmus' differing commitment, his "philosophy of Christ." Luther abhors and ignores the Renaissance search for Christian Humanism, and he is furiously suspicious of Erasmus' intellectuality ("Du bist nicht fromm!"). The Renaissance Church had pulled the world to herself, art, reason, science, life. Luther's religious seriousness and polemics against the "reason of this world" helped decisively in cutting this Renaissance Church wide open. What is more important, tolerance or commitment? Where is truth?

The two protagonists become symbolic for two camps, unable to meet. Erasmus defines free will: "By freedom of the will we understand in this connection the power of the human will whereby man can apply to or turn away from that which leads unto eternal salvation." Luther says that man is unable to do anything but continue to sin, except for God's grace. The whole work of man's salvation, first to last, is God's. Both proceed from different vantage points. Erasmus dismisses both the excessive confidence in man's moral strength, held by the Pelagians, and what he believed to be St. Augustine's view, the excessive hopelessness of a final condemnation passed on man. He identified Luther with the latter. Erasmus calls Scripture to help in outlining his reasonable and conciliatory middle way, really a philosophical and pragmatic statement of man's essential freedom. Luther interprets this to mean assigning free will to divine things, because his interest lies in practical implementation of a classical Christian paradox, which he thought solved. His solution is "faith alone sets us free."

Consult the footnotes (especially I/1; III/2,3/10,11; V/8). Erasmus tries to skirt the difficulties that Luther's problematic mind discovers in much of the Church's age old interpretation of this Christian paradox.

Modern commentators recognize dimly in Erasmus a budding interest in theodicy. With it he influenced thinkers for the next centuries (especially from Leibnitz to Kant). His definition of free will "lives," because it is for the sake of "living man." Already in his *Antibarbari,* a defense of good learning in a Platonic setting, written while still in the monastery, Erasmus makes a keen distinction between two spheres of human existence, one based on pious faith and the other on critical scholarship. For him man is the *only* being who is capable of being at one and the same time moral and scientific. Luther, fiery and committed, is really interested in the grace of God. Erasmus seeks the theological and intellectual virtues in the dawning modern age.

* * *

The original of Erasmus has no subheadings or paragraphs. The chapter and subheadings here used follow in the main the division of the work, as acknowledged by Luther and others.

Special thanks are due to Professors Paul Oskar Kristeller and Frederick W. Locke and to Reverend Herbert Musurillo for reading the entire manuscript and for making valuable suggestions. To the publishers, for their constructive comments on the manuscript and their care in producing this volume, my added appreciation. For any errors, none but the translator is responsible.

ERNST F. WINTER

SELECTED BIBLIOGRAPHY

MORTIMER JEROME ADLER, *The Idea of Freedom:* A Dialectical Examination of the Conception of Freedom, New York, Doubleday, 1958

LOUIS BOUYER, C.O., *Erasmus and His Times,* tr. by F. X. Murphy, C.Ss.R., Westminster, Md., Newman, 1959

E. CASSIRER, P.O. KRISTELLER, J.H. RANDALL, JR., *The Renaissance Philosophy of Man,* University of Chicago Press, 1948 (1956)

ERIK H. ERIKSON, *Young Man Luther:* A Study in Psychoanalysis and History, New York, Norton, 1958

JOHANNES HESSEN, *Luther in katholischer Sicht,* Grundlegung eines ökumenischen Gespräches, Bonn, L. Röhrscheid, 1949

JOHAN HUIZINGA, *Erasmus and the Age of Reformation,* New York, Harper, 1924 (1957)

PIERRE MESNARD, *Erasme de Rotterdam,* essai sur le libre arbitre, Algiers, R. Chaix, 1945

J. I. PACKER AND O. R. JOHNSTON, *Martin Luther on the Bondage of the Will,* Westwood, N.J., F.H. Revell, 1958

MARGARET MANN PHILLIPS, *Erasmus and the Northern Renaissance,* London, Hodder & Stoughton, 1949

CONTENTS

Part I ERASMUS: *The Free Will*

Part II LUTHER: *The Bondage of the Will*

Part One

ERASMUS

THE FREE WILL

I

A DIATRIBE OR SERMON
CONCERNING FREE WILL

Desiderius Erasmus of Rotterdam

PREFACE: MAN AND TRUTH

AMONG the many difficulties encountered in Holy Scripture
—and there are many of them—none presents a more per-
plexed labyrinth than the problem of the freedom of the
will. In ancient and more recent times philosophers and
theologians[1] have been vexed by it to an astonishing degree,

[1] Arguments criticizing the free will are easier to find and to present than those in its defense and explanation. Early Greek views
were already varied and obscure. The *Eleatics, Democritus* and the
Stoics generally opposed the freedom of the will. The *Pythagoreans,
Socrates, Plato, Aristotle* and *Epicurus* attempted various explana-
tions in its defense. Cf. Dom David Amand, *Fatalism et liberté dans
l'antiquité grecque,* Louvain, 1945. Socrates and Plato held that the
good, being identical with the true, imposes itself irresistably on the
will and the intellect, once it is clearly known and understood. Evil
results from ignorance. Aristotle disagrees partly and appeals to experience. Vice is voluntary. Chance plays a role in some actions.
The irresistible influence of his Prime Mover, however, makes the
conception of a genuine moral freedom a difficulty for him. Epicurus advocated free will, in order to assuage man's fear caused by
belief in irresistible fate.
Medieval thought developed a complex theology of the free will.
Preeminent among the theologians is *St. Augustine of Hippo* who
taught the freedom of the will against the Manichaeans, but the
necessity of grace against the Pelagians. This two-fold apologetic
gave rise later to interpretation differences, of which the Erasmus-
Luther controversy is just one example. *St. Thomas Aquinas* developed some aspects of Augustine's teachings. Will is rational
appetite. Free will becomes simply the elective power for choosing

but, as it seems to me, with more exertion than success on their part. Recently, Carlstadt and Eck restored interest in the problem, debating it, however, with moderation.[2] Soon thereafter, Martin Luther took up the whole controversy once more—and in a rather heated fashion—with his formal *Assertion* concerning the freedom of the will.[3] And

---

different forms of desired beatitudes. How are man's future acts not necessary, despite God's infallible prevision? God does not exist in time: past and future alike are ever present. How about God's omnipotent providence? Does it infringe on man's freedom by its perfect control over all happenings? Two schools of thought among the Scholastics, both logically continuing certain of Aquinas' teachings, came to the fore. This Scholasticism irritated both Erasmus and Luther. It developed the finer points, often ignored by Erasmus and challenged by Luther's assertions. The Dominican or Thomist school saw God as premoving man in accord with his free nature. Divine foreknowledge and God's providential control of the world's history are in harmony with man, who is by nature and definition a free cause. Animals are not. They are in harmony with their nature, adopting particular courses by necessity. The Jesuit or Molinist school does not think this explains freedom of the human will sufficiently. They conceive the relation of divine action to man's will to be concurrent rather than promotive, exempting God more clearly from all responsibility for man's sin.

Some of the complexity with which generations of thinkers have been grappling can be found in the Erasmus-Luther debate. In a sense it is a disorganized summary of the classical and medieval debates. Thereafter, beginning perhaps with Spinoza, a new rationalism enters the debate. Of this Erasmus is something of a precursor, exuding reasonableness on his part. For an up-to-date presentation of the entire panorama, see Mortimer J. Adler, *The Idea of Freedom*: A Dialectical Examination of the Conception of Freedom (see Biblography).

---

[2] *Andreas Carlstadt* (1480-1541), a pioneer of the Protestant Reformation, was asked by Luther to defend his Thesis of 1517 at a public disputation ("Divine grace and human free will") at the University of Leipzig (June 27, 1519). He later came to oppose Luther as a "compromiser."

Johann Maier von Eck (1486-1543), German Catholic theologian, challenged Carlstadt to this debate. He remained foremost among those working for the overthrow of Luther.

[3] Erasmus refers to *Assertio omnium articulorum D. Mart. Luth. per bullam Leonis X damnatorum* (1520) in the Weimar edition

although more than one[4] has answered his *Assertion*, I, too, encouraged by my friends, am going to try to see whether, by the following brief discussion, the truth might not become more visible.

1) *Luther's Supposed Infallibility*

Here some will surely close their ears and exclaim, "Oh prodigy! Erasmus dares to contend with Luther, a fly with an elephant?" In order to assuage such people, I only want to state at this point, if they give me the time for it, that I have actually never sworn allegiance to the words of Luther. Nobody should therefore consider it unseemly if I should openly disagree with him, if nothing else, as one man from another. It is therefore by no means an outrage to dispute over one of his dogmas, especially not, if one, in order to discover truth, confronts Luther with calm and scholarly arguments. I certainly believe that Luther will not feel hurt if somebody differs in some instances from his opinion, because he permits himself not only to argue against the decisions of all the doctors of the church, but

---

of Luther's works (henceforth referred to as *W.A.*, i.e., *Weimarer Ausgabe*), *W.A.* VII, p. 91 ff. Luther himself seems to have preferred his freer German rendition, *Grund und Ursache aller Artikel D. Martin Luther, so durch römische Bulle unrechtlich verdammt sind, W.A.* VII, p. 309 ff. Article 36, restating the 13th Heidelberg thesis, asserts that the free will is a mere fiction. Article 31 asserts that a pious man sins doing good works. Article 32 asserts that a good work is a mortal sin. Cf. chapter IV, footnote 5.

---

[4] Among the major tracts against Luther we find, besides Eck's *Obelisci* (1518), the following: Henry VIII, *Assertio septem sacramentorum* (1521), which earned him the title Defender of the Faith; St. Thomas More, *Eruditissimi vivi Gul. Rossi opus legans quo pulcherrime retegit ac refellit insanas Lutheri calumnias* (1523), written at the request of Henry VIII, in answer to Luther's reply to the royal *Assertio;* St. John Fisher, *The sermon of Iohan the bysshop of Rochester made agayn ye peverisyous doctryn of Martin Luther* (1521), on which Erasmus relied heavily. Cf. chapter VI, footnote 1.

also appeals against all schools, church councils and Popes. Since he asserts this freely and openly, his friends must not hold it against me if I do likewise.

2) *Objectivity and Scepticism*

Let no one misinterpret our battle. We are not two gladiators incited against each other. I want to argue only against one of Luther's teachings, illuminating, if this be possible, in the subsequent clash of scriptural passages and arguments, the truth, the investigation of which has always been the most reputable activity of scholars. There will be no invective, and for two reasons: it does not behoove Christians so to act; and moreover, the truth, which by excessive quarreling is often lost, is discovered with greater certainty without it.

I am quite aware that I am a poor match in such a contest; I am less experienced than other men, and I have always had a deep-seated aversion to fighting. Consequently I have always preferred playing in the freer field of the muses, than fighting ironclad in close combat. In addition, so great is my dislike of assertions that I prefer the views of the sceptics wherever the inviolable authority of Scripture and the decision of the Church permit—a Church to which at all times I willingly submit my own views, whether I attain what she prescribes or not. And as a matter of fact, I prefer this natural inclination to one I can observe in certain people who are so blindly addicted to one opinion that they cannot tolerate whatever differs from it. Whatever they read in Holy Scripture, they distort to serve the opinion to which they have once and for all enslaved themselves. Their case is like that of the young man who loves a girl so much that he fancies he sees her image everywhere. Or to use a better comparison: they are like those who in the heat of battle turn everything at hand, be it a pitcher or a plate, into a missile. Are people thus affected able to form an objective judgment? Or is it not rather the result of such disputations that both contestants part spitting upon each other in contempt? There will always be many such people, the kind the Apostle Peter describes as, "the unlearned and the unstable," such as "distort the Scriptures to their own destruction" (2 Peter 3,16).

3) *Having an Open Mind*

For these reasons then, I must confess that I have not yet formed a definite opinion on any of the numerous traditional views regarding the freedom of the will; all I am willing to assert is that the will enjoys some power of freedom. My reading of Martin Luther's *Assertion* was quite unprejudiced, except that I felt towards him a favor such as a lawyer feels towards a hard pressed defendant. Though Luther's argument is defended with every means at his disposal and presented with great verve, I must honestly confess that he has not yet convinced me.

If someone wishes to declare me slow-witted or ignorant on account of all this, I would not want to argue the point, provided it is permitted for intellectually weaker persons to argue with better endowed ones for the sake of learning. Moreover, Luther himself attributed very little to erudition, but a great deal to the Spirit who instills at times in the intellectually weak what he denies to the wise. This I am saying to those who loudly proclaim that Luther has more learning in his little finger than Erasmus in his entire body —which I am not now going to refute. As hostile as those people wish to be in this affair, they will have to admit that my case shall not be weakened by the judgment of a few foolhardy people, if I concede to Luther in this disputation that he should not be burdened with the preceding judgment of doctors, councils, scholars, popes and emperors. Even if I have understood what Luther discusses, it is altogether possible that I am mistaken. Therefore, I merely want to analyze and not to judge, to inquire and not to dogmatize. I am ready to learn from anyone who advances something more accurate or more reliable, though I would

rather persuade mediocre minds not to argue too stubbornly
on such matters. It harms Christian concord more than it
helps piety.

4) *Difficulties in the Scripture*

Holy Scripture contains secrets into which God does not
want us to penetrate too deeply, because if we attempt to
do so, increasing darkness envelopes us, so that we might
come to recognize in this manner both the unfathomable
majesty of divine wisdom and the feebleness of the human
mind. Pomponius Mela, for instance, speaks of a certain
Corycian grotto[5] which at first entices intruders by its
charm, and later frightens them and fills them with terror
because of the majesty of the indwelling divinity. Consequently, when we have reached such a point, I think it
prudent and more pious to exclaim with Paul, "Oh, the
depth of the riches of the wisdom and of the knowledge
of God! How incomprehensible are his judgments and how
unsearchable his ways!" (Romans 11,33), and with Isaiah,
"Who hath forwarded the spirit of the Lord? Or who hath
been his counselor?" (Isaiah 40,13), rather than to try to
explain what surpasses the measure of the human mind.
Much will have to wait for that time when we shall see no
longer in a mirror and in an enigma, but shall contemplate
in its glory the unveiled face of the Lord.

5) *Essence of Christian Piety*

In my opinion the implications of the freedom of the
will in Holy Scripture are as follows: if we are on the road
to piety, we should continue to improve eagerly and forget
what lies behind us; if we have become involved in sin,
we should make every effort to extricate ourselves, to
accept the remedy of penance, and to solicit the mercy of

[5] Pomponius Mela, Spanish geographer in the first century *AD*
and author of an early universal geography, *De situ orbis*. The
Corycian Cave, or "cave of myth," is a stalactite grotto on the
southern slope of Mt. Parnassus, near Delphi, Greece, and played
a role in Greek mythology.

the Lord, without which neither the human will nor its striving is effective; for all evil let us consider ourselves responsible, but let us ascribe all good to Divine Benevolence alone, for to It we owe even what we are; and in all things must we believe that whatever delightful or sad happens to us during life, God has caused it for our salvation, and that no injustice can come from Him who is by nature just, even if something should befall us which we deem undeserved; nobody should despair of forgiveness by a God who is by nature most merciful. In my opinion, it used to be sufficient for Christian piety to cling to these truths.

6) *Man's Limited Capacity to Know*

Men were not wont to intrude upon these concealed, even superfluous questions with irreligious curiosity, namely, whether God's foreknowledge is contingent; whether our will can contribute anything to our eternal salvation, or whether it simply undergoes the action of operative grace; whether everything we do, good or evil, is done out of mere necessity, or whether we are rather in a state of passive acceptance. Some things God wishes to remain totally unknown to us, such as the day of our death and the day of the last judgment. "It is not for you to know the times or dates which the Father has fixed by his own power" (Acts 1,7). Or, "But of the day or hour no one knows, neither the angels in heaven, nor the Son, but the Father only" (Mark 13,32).

In other instances God wishes that we investigate by venerating Him in mystic silence. Therefore Holy Scripture contains numerous passages which have puzzled many, without ever anyone succeeding in completely clarifying them. For example, there is the question of the distinction of the persons in God; the union of the divine and human natures in Christ; the problem of irremissible sin.[6]

Other things He wanted us to know with the utmost

---

[6] Mark 3, 29.

clarity, as for example, the precepts for a morally good life. This is obviously the word of God which one does not have to fetch down from high heaven, or a distant sea, but which one rather finds near at hand, namely in our mouths and in our hearts.[7] This indeed must be learned well by all. The remaining is better committed to God. It is more devout to adore the unknown than to investigate the unexplorable. How many quarrels have arisen from investigations into the distinction of persons in the Holy Trinity, the manner of procession of the Holy Spirit, the virgin birth? What disturbances have been caused in the world by the fierce contentions concerning the conception of the virgin mother of God? What are the results of these laborious investigations except that we experience a great loss of concord, and love each other less, while we wish to know too much?

Besides, there are certain kinds of truth which, even though they could be known, would nonetheless be unwisely offered for indiscriminate consideration. Perhaps what the sophists used to say about God, that, given his nature, he is present as much in the cavity of a beetle as in heaven, has some truth to it (I blush to reproduce their actual shameful remark).[8] It would be unprofitable to discuss this matter publicly. Furthermore, the assertion that there are three gods, even if it can be truly stated dialectically, would certainly cause great offense, if presented to the untutored masses. Were I certain—which is not the case—that confession, as we have it now, was neither instituted by Christ, nor could ever have been invented by man, and consequently nobody could require it, and that furthermore no satisfaction is needed for offenses committed, I would nonetheless fear to publicize such an opinion, because, from what I can see, most men are prone to moral turpitude. Now, obligatory confession restrains or at least moderates this propensity.[9] There exist certain sicknesses of the body

---

[7]   Deuteronomy 30, 11-14 and Romans 10, 6-8.

[8]   Luther, as well as Erasmus, criticized some Scholastics as "sophists," i.e., those well versed in specious reasoning and arguments.

[9]   Luther strongly criticized confession.

which it is the lesser evil to bear than to remove, as for example, if we had to bathe in the warm blood of slaughtered children in order to remove leprosy. There are, indeed, errors which it is better to ignore, than to eliminate. Paul has differentiated between the permissible and the expedient.[10] The truth may be spoken but it does not serve everyone at all times and under all circumstances. If I were certain that a wrong decision or definition had been reached at a synod, it would be permissible but not expedient to speak the truth concerning it. Wicked men should not thus be offered an occasion to disdain the authority of the Fathers, especially when they have conscientiously and scrupulously made decisions. I would prefer to say that at the time of the decision they acted on the evidence they had, and later practical exigencies persuade us to modify their judgments.

7) *Unsuitableness of Luther's Teachings*

Let us assume the truth of what Wycliffe[11] has taught and Luther has asserted, namely, that everything we do happens not on account of our free will, but out of sheer necessity. What could be more useless than to publish this paradox to the world? Secondly, let us assume that it is true, as Augustine has written somewhere, that God causes both good and evil in us,[12] and that he rewards us for his good works wrought in us and punishes us for the evil deeds done in us. What a loophole the publication of this opinion would open to godlessness among innumerable people? In particular: mankind is lazy, indolent, malicious, and, in addition, incorrigibly prone to every impious outrage. How many weak ones would continue in their perpetual and

---

[10]   1 Corinthians 2, 1-6. Erasmus prefers throughout using the Latin for "expedient," rather than the word "prudential."

[11]   John Wycliffe (1330-1384), one of the early influential English reformers tried, as a philosophical realist, to explain predestination and free will.

[12]   Erasmus was admittedly not well versed in Augustinian theology and philosophy.

laborious battle against their own flesh? What wicked fellow would henceforth try to better his conduct? Who could love with all his heart a God who fires a hell with eternal pain, in order to punish there poor mankind for his own evil deeds, as if God enjoyed human distress? Most people would react as they are sketched above. People are universally ignorant and carnal-minded. They tend towards unbelief, wickedness and blasphemy. There is no sense in pouring oil upon the fire.

Thus Paul, the prudent disburser of the divine word, frequently consults charity and prefers to pursue what serves the neighbor, rather than what is permissible. Among the mature he speaks with the wisdom he possesses. But before the weak he displays no other knowledge but that of Jesus Christ, the crucified.[13] Holy Scripture knows how to adjust its language to our human condition. In it are passages where God is angry, grieved, indignant, furious; where he threatens and hates. Again in other places he has mercy, he regrets, he changes his intentions. This does not mean that such changes really take place in the nature of God. These are rather modes of expression, benefitting our weakmindedness and dullness. The same prudence should, I believe, adorn all who have taken up preaching the divine word. Some things can be noxious, because like wine for the feverish, they are not fitting. Hence such matters might be treated in discourses among the educated or also in theological schools, although it is not expedient even there I think unless done with caution. Definitely, it seems to me, it is not only unsuitable, but truly pernicious to carry on such disputations when everybody can listen.

In short, one should be persuaded to waste neither time nor ingenuity in such labyrinths; neither to refute nor to endorse Luther's teachings. Perhaps I deserve the reproach of having been too verbose in this preface. But all of it appears more important than the disputation proper.

---

[13]　1 Corinthians 2, 1-6.

II

INTRODUCTION:
OBJECTIVE CRITERION FOR
TRUTH

Since Luther recognizes no authority of any author, however approved, except that of the canonical books, I gladly accept this diminution of labor. Both among the Greeks and the Latins exist innumerable thinkers who deal explicitly or cursorily with the freedom of the will. It would have been a formidable task to gather all the quotations for and against free will; to explain every passage as well as to refute it. This irksome exertion would have been wasted on Luther and his friends, particularly since they not only hold different opinions, but also contradict themselves extensively.

8) *Authority of the Church Fathers*

Nevertheless I wish to remind the reader, if he thinks we are holding the scale to Luther's, with our scriptural passages and firm reasoning, that he now visualize in addition the entire long list of most erudite men who have enjoyed the approval of many centuries up to the present day, and among whom most have distinguished themselves by an admirable knowledge of Scripture, and commended themselves by their piety. Some gave their lives as testimony to the teachings of Christ which they had defended in their writings. Such among the Greeks are: Origen, Basil, Chrysostom, Cyril, John Damascene and Theophylactus; among the Latins: Tertullian, Cyprian, Arnobius, Hilary, Jerome and Augustine. I could also mention Thomas

13

Aquinas, Duns Scotus, Durandus of Saint-Pourçain, John Capreolus, Gabriel Biel, Giles of Rome, Gregory of Rimini and Alexander of Hales.[1] Their powerful and subtle argumentation, in my opinion, nobody can completely disdain, not to speak of the authoritative decisions of many universities, councils and popes.

From Apostolic times to this day no author has hitherto completely denied the freedom of the will, save Manichaeus and John Wycliffe alone.[2] Lorenzo Valla's authority, who

---

[1]   *Origen* (185-254) was one of the most prolific writers of the early Church. His interests in Platonism and in giving philosophy a recognized place in the creeds of the Church made him a controversial figure. Erasmus was particularly influenced by his scriptural commentaries.

St. Basil the Great (330-? 379-?), early Church Father, as was *St. John Chrysostom* (344?-407). *St. Cyril* (315?-386?), bishop of Jerusalem. *St. John of Damascus* (675-749), theologian and doctor of the Eastern Church. *Quintus Septimius Florens Tertullianus* (160?-230?), ecclesiastical writer and creator of Christian Latin literature, was one of the most original and controversial Christian writers. He influenced Erasmus. *St. Cyprian* (200-258), African bishop; *St. Hilary* (died 367), bishop of Poitiers, France; *St. Ambrose of Milan* (339-397), Latin Church Father. *St. Jerome* (340-420) is best known for his classical translation of the Old, and revision of the New Testament, known as the *Vulgate Bible. St. Augustine of Hippo* (354-430), bishop and Church Father. *St. Thomas Aquinas* (1225-1274), theologian and philosopher, called the Angelic Doctor. *Duns Scotus* (1265?-1308?), medieval theologian at Oxford and Cologne. *Durandus of Saint-Pourçain* (d. 1332), philosopher and theologian with a vast literary production, known as Doctor resolutissimus. *John Capreolus* (d. 1444), theologian, called Prince of Thomists. *Gabriel Biel* (d. 1495), German scholastic philosopher, influenced Luther and Melanchthon. *Giles of Rome* (1245-1316), Italian theologian and philosopher, called Doctor fundatissimus. *Alexander of Hales* (d. 1245), English philosopher and theologian.

[2]   *Manichaeus,* Mani or Manes (his followers are called *Manichaeans*) was a Gnostic teacher (d. 273), preaching an eclectic creed composed of wild fancies and some Hebrew, Buddhist, and Christian concepts, centering around the realms of light and darkness, good and evil. Augustine was for nine years a Manichaean, preceding his conversion to Christianity.

almost seems to agree with them, has little weight among theologians.[3] Manichaeus' teaching has always been sharply rejected by all the world. Yet, it is questionable whether it would not serve better than Wycliffe's. The former explains good and evil by the two natures in man, but in such a way that we owe the good acts to God on account of his creation, and because we can, despite the power of darkness, implore the creator for help. This can help us to sin less and to do good more readily. If everything reduces itself to pure necessity, where does Wycliffe leave us any room for prayer or our own striving?

To return to what I have been saying before. Once the reader of my disputation recognizes that my fighting equipment is equal to that of the adversary, let him decide for himself, whether to attribute more to the decisions of all the many scholars, orthodox faithful, saints, martyrs, theologians of ancient and more recent times; of all the universities, as well as of the many councils, bishops and popes, or more to the private opinions of one or two men. I don't want to make the number of voices or the rank of the speakers decide an issue, as is customary in human assemblies. I know it happens frequently that the better party is voted down by the majority. I know what the majority esteems is not always the best. I know, when investigating truth, there is no harm in adding to the diligence of one's predecessors. I admit that it is right that the sole authority of Holy Scripture surpasses the voices of all mortals.

But we are not involved in a controversy regarding Scripture. The same Scripture is being loved and revered by both parties. Our battle concerns the sense of Scripture. If

---

[3]   *Lorenzo Valla* (1405-1457) was foremost among Italian Humanists. He, too, wrote a dialogue on free will. See Cassirer et al., *The Renaissance Philosophy of Man,* University of Chicago Press, 1948 pp. 147-182. Both Erasmus and Luther claimed him. In a sense Valla anticipated Erasmus, Ulrich von Hutten, and Luther in his philosophical, critical and exegetical works. (*Ibid.,* p. 154). Erasmus edited Valla's *Annotationes in Novum Testamentum,* critical of the Vulgate's version.

ingenuity and erudition contribute anything to scriptural interpretation, what could be more acute and perspicacious than the Greek mind? How about wide scriptural reading? Nor have the Latins been wanting in either. If they were by nature less fruitful than the Greeks, they equaled them in industriousness and accepted their helpful inheritance. If, on the other hand, one looks more to a virtuous course of life than to erudition, it is obvious which men stand on the side of free will. Let us set aside what the lawyers call an odious comparison. I do not wish to compare some heralds of this new gospel with the older ones.

9) *Inspiration by the Holy Spirit*

At this point someone may object: what is the need of an interpreter when Scripture itself is quite clear? If it is really so clear, why have all the excellent people here acted like blind men for so many centuries, especially in so important a matter as my opponents hold it to be? If nothing were dark in Scripture, what need for prophecy was there even during apostolic times? This was the gift of the Spirit. Now, it is questionable whether this charismatic gift has ceased, like the power to heal and the gift of tongues did cease. If it did not cease, one has to ask, to whom was it transferred? If this talent and grace of prophecy have been transferred to everybody, any interpretation becomes highly problematical; if to nobody, we would still not have an assured interpretation, since even scholars are toiling with obscurities; if to the successors of the Apostles, then they will object that many of them completely lacked the apostolic spirit. And yet, other things being equal, we can presume with greater probability that God communicated His Spirit to those who have been ordained, just as one considers it more probable that grace will flow to the baptized, rather than to the non-baptized.

Let us admit that the possibility actually exists for the Spirit to reveal to a simple layman what is not revealed to many scholars, since indeed Christ thanks His Father for revealing to little ones,[4] that is, those simple and foolish in the eyes of this world,[5] what He concealed from the wise and prudent ones, that is, the scribes, pharisees, and philosophers. Dominic and Francis might have been such fools, if they could have followed their own spirit. But since St. Paul during his own lifetime, when the gift of the Spirit was alive, had already to order His verification, that is, whether His manifestation really came from God,[6] what shall happen during our worldly times? How can we judge the Spirit? According to erudition? On both sides we find scribes. According to conduct? On both sides there are sinners. True, on one side stands the entire choir of saints who steadfastly held to the freedom of the will. They state the truth, but they were human. Yet I am comparing men to men, instead of men to God.

If it is objected: what can large numbers contribute to an understanding of the Spirit? I answer: what can a small number of people? If they object: what can a bishop's miter contribute to an understanding of Holy Scripture? I answer: what can a hood and cowl? If they say: what can philosophical understanding contribute? I answer: what can ignorance? If they say: what can a congregated synod, in which perhaps nobody is inspired by the Spirit, contribute to an understanding of Scripture? I answer: what can the private gathering of a few contribute, none of whom probably has the Spirit?

10) *Miracles and Exemplary Life*

Paul exclaims, "Do you seek a proof of the Christ who speaks in me?" (2 Corinthians 13,3). Apostles were believed only if their doctrines were accompanied by miracles. But nowadays anybody demands faith from others by affirming his having the evangelical spirit. The apostles had to rout vipers, heal the sick, raise the dead, confer the gift of

---

[4]   Matthew 11, 25.
[5]   1 Corinthians 1, 27.
[6]   1 Corinthians 12, 3; words are actually taken from 1 John 4, 1.

tongues by the laying on of hands. Only thus were they believed and hardly even thus, since they taught paradoxes. Nowadays certain people present even greater paradoxes[7] to common opinion! Nonetheless, none of them has come forward who could heal just one lame horse. If at least some of them would demonstrate, not quite a miracle, but yet the sincerity and simplicity of an apostolic life, it could take the place of the missing miracle amongst us more slow-witted people.

I do not want to accuse Luther, whom I don't know personally, but whose writings have made a mixed impression on me. I am addressing this to others who are better known to me and who interrupt us by saying, "They were simply men," every time we advance an interpretation by an orthodox elder for the purpose of understanding a controversial passage. When we ask, what are the marks of a true scriptural interpretation, since both sides are represented only by human beings, their answer is "The mark of the Holy Spirit." If you ask why the Holy Spirit should have forsaken the side which is also distinguished by miracles, and be found rather amongst them, they answer as if during all these hundreds of years there had been no Gospel in the world. If one misses among them a conduct of life commensurate with the Spirit, they answer that they are saved by faith and not by works. If one misses miracles, they say these have stopped long ago and are no longer needed, since now the light of Scripture shines so wonderfully. If one contests that Scripture is clear in our case, otherwise so many excellent men would also have been blind, one has moved in a full cycle to the beginning of the argument.

11) *Infallible Church*

Let us assume that he who has the Spirit is sure of the meaning of Scripture. How can I also possess the certainty which the other pretends to have? What can I do when

---

[7] Luther called his 1517 theses "theological paradoxa."

several persons claim different interpretations, but each one swears to have the Spirit? Moreover, since the Spirit does not inspire the same person with everything, some who have the Spirit may be mistaken on a point.

This then I want to reply to those who discard without hesitation the old interpretation of sacred books, and instead submit their own, as if an oracle had proclaimed it. Finally, even though Christ's Spirit might permit His people to be in error in an unimportant question on which man's salvation does not depend, no one could believe that this Spirit has deliberately overlooked error in His Church for 1300 years, and that He did not deem one of all the pious and saintly Church Fathers worthy enough to be inspired, with what, they contend, is the very essence of all evangelical teaching.

12) *Plea for Gentle Listening*

But now, in order finally to conclude, let the others decide what they wish to assume for themselves. I for my part do not arrogate to myself doctrine, nor sanctity, nor do I depend on my intellect. I simply want to offer with earnestness what moves my soul. If someone undertakes to teach me, I would not consciously oppose truth. If my opponents, however, prefer to slander me, although I dispute truthfully and without slander, rather than quarrel, then everyone will miss the Spirit of the Gospels among those who continuously speak of it. Paul exhorts, "But him who is weak in faith, receive" (Romans 14,1). Christ will not extinguish a smoking wick.[8] The Apostle Peter says, "Be ready always with an answer to everyone who asks a reason for the hope that is in you. Yet, do so with gladness and fear" (1 Peter 3,15-16). If my opponents respond, "Erasmus is like an old wine-skin[9] unable to hold the new wine which they offer to the world," and if their self-confidence is so great, they at least ought to consider us as Christ did

---

[8] Matthew 12, 20.
[9] Matthew 9, 17.

Nicodemus,[10] and as the Apostles did Gamaliel.[11] The Lord did not repel the former, who, though ignorant, was desirous of learning. Nor did the Apostles spurn Gamaliel who desired to suspend his judgment until the nature of the matter would show by what spirit it was being led.

13) *Definition of Free Will*

I have completed half of this work. To those whom I have convinced, as I intended, that it were better not to cavil and quibble about such questions, especially not before the common people, I will not have to present the further proof to which I shall now proceed, hoping that truth will prevail everywhere, which will perhaps sparkle from a comparison of scriptural passages like fire struck from flint. Nobody can deny that Sacred Scripture contains many passages stating the obvious freedom of the human will. On the other hand, there are some passages which seem to deny the former. Yet, it is certatin that Scripture cannot contradict itself, since all passages are inspired by the same Spirit. Therefore, we shall first examine those passages which confirm our view and then we shall try to dispose of those that seem to be opposed.

By freedom of the will we understand in this connection the power of the human will whereby man can apply to or turn away from that which leads unto eternal salvation.

---

[10]   John 3.
[11]   Acts 5, 34.

III

OLD TESTAMENT PROOFS
SUPPORTING THE FREE WILL

14) *Ecclesiasticus 15: Choose Good or Evil*

Those who take a free will for granted usually quote
Ecclesiasticus 15, 14-18:

> *God made man from the beginning, and left him in the
> hand of his own counsel. He added his commandment and
> precepts. If thou wilt keep the commandments and per-
> form acceptable fidelity forever, they shall preserve thee.
> He hath set water and fire before thee; stretch forth thy
> hand to which thou wilt. Before man is life and death,
> good and evil, that which he shall choose shall be given
> him.*

I do not expect that anybody will question the authority
of this book because it was of old not contained in the
Hebraic canon, as Jerome indicates. The Church of Christ
has received it into her canon with great unanimity. Incidentally, I do not quite see why the Hebrews decided to
exclude it from their canon, while at the same time including Solomon's Proverbs and the Canticle of Canticles. Whoever has read attentively can readily guess why the Jews
excluded from their canon the last two books of Esdras,
the story of Susanna and of the dragon Bel, attached to the
book of Daniel, as well as the books Judith and Esther and
a few others. They numbered these among the apocrypha.[1]
But in Ecclesiasticus certainly nothing disturbs the reader.

---

[1] *Apocrypha,* a term used to describe that body of religious literature closely associated with the Old and New Testament, but regarded as noncanonical Jewish or Christian scriptures.

15) *Adam and Eve*

The above passage then makes us realize that Adam, the first man, was created with an uncorrupted reason which could distinguish between the desirable and the sinful. In addition, he had received also an uncorrupted will, but which remained quite free, if he wished, to choose also evil. All the angels were created in the same way before the revolt against God by Lucifer and his followers. Afterwards, in those angels who fell, the will was so completely corrupted, that they could not perform any meritorious act. In those who remained faithful, their good will was so strengthened that it became henceforth impossible for them to choose evil. In man, will was so good and so free that even without additional grace it could have remained in a state of innocence, though not without the help of grace could it attain the blessedness of eternal life, as the Lord Jesus promised his people. Even if all this cannot be proved by clear scriptural testimony, it has been expounded with good foundation by orthodox Church Fathers. Incidentally, in Eve obviously not only the will was weakened, but also reason and intellect, the fountain of all good or all evil. It seems that the snake succeeded in persuading her that the Lord's prohibition to eat from the tree of life was vain. In Adam it seems rather that the will was weakened more because of his immoderate love for his wife to whose desires he gave preference over obedience to God's commandments. Yet also his reason had, I think, been weakened, which is the source of the will.

16) *Man before and after Receiving Grace; Reason and Revelation*

Our power of judgment—whether we call it *nous,* i.e., mind or intellect, or rather *logos,* i.e., reason—has only been obscured by sin, and not extinguished. Our will, considered as ability to choose or to avoid, had thus been worsened to a degree, so that it could not improve itself by its own natural means; it had lost its freedom and was obliged to serve the sin to which it once willingly assented. But, by the grace of God which forgives sin, the freedom of the will has been restored to such a degree that according to the Pelagians eternal life can now be gained even without the help of further grace.[2] This happens in such a manner that, first, one owes his salvation to the will of God, who both created and restored free will; and according to the orthodox, because of the help of divine grace, which always aids his effort, man can persevere in the right state without, however, being freed of his propensity to evil, which stems from the remains of sin once committed. Just as the sin of our first parents was passed on to their descendants, so we also inherited the propensity to sin. Sin-absolving grace can to a degree aid in our overcoming of sin, but not extirpate it. Not that grace could not accomplish this, but because it does not profit us.

In those without extraordinary grace[3] the reason is darkened, but not extinguished. Probably the same occurs to the power of the will: it is not completely extinct, but unproductive of virtuous deeds. What the eyes are for the body, reason is for the soul. Reason is partly illumined by an innate light inborn in us, though not in equal measure in all, as the psalmist sings: "Raise the light of thy countenance above us, O Lord!" (Psalm 4,7). And reason is partly illumined by divine precepts and Holy Scripture,

---

[2] *Pelagius,* a British monk of the late 4th and early 5th centuries *AD,* was a contemporary of Augustine. His followers were known as Pelagians. His doctrine, Pelagianism, taught that the will is free only when influenced neither toward good nor toward evil. Man is endowed with original perfection. Augustine formed his own views on original sin and divine grace in opposition to Pelagianism, declared heretical by the Church Council of Ephesus (431). The *Semi-Pelagians* of the later 5th century taught a modified form, condemned in 529. Erasmus' interpretation of Pelagianism is less critical than that of the Church. Luther thus inclines to classify Erasmus as a Pelagian, something he distinctly abhors.

[3] Extraordinary grace (*gratia peculiaris*) prepared, according to the Scholastics, for the reception of final sanctifying grace. Cf. also footnote 11.

wherefore our psalmist sings,[4] "Thy words are a light to my footsteps."

17) *Law of Nature, Law of Good Works, Law of Faith*

Therefore we are born under three kinds of laws: the law of nature, the law of good works, and the law of faith, to use Paul's expression.[5]

The Law of Nature, carved deeply into the minds of all, tells Scythians as well as Greeks that it is unjust to do to another what one does not wish to suffer himself. Without the help of Scripture and without the light of faith, philosophers have gained a knowledge of divine kindness and greatness by observing the created world. They have left us many moral precepts which bear an astounding resemblance to the precepts of the Gospels. We possess many of their sayings, encouraging virtue and detesting turpitude. Thus it seems probable that they had a will tending to moral good, but incapable of eternal salvation, unless grace be added through faith.

The Law of Good Works, on the other hand, issues commands and sanctions them with punishment. It increases sin and causes death, not because it is evil, but because it requires good works which, without grace, we could not possibly perform.

The Law of Faith which, posing even more difficult commandments than the law of works, makes what would be impossible, not only easy but also pleasant, as long as we are supported by abundant grace. Thus faith heals our reason which has suffered through sin, and charity helps our weakened will to act.

To a certain extent the Law of Good Works was expressed in Genesis 2,16, "From every tree of the garden you may eat; but from the tree of the knowledge of good and evil you must not eat; for the day you eat of it, you

---

[4]   Erasmus' text states Psalm 113. Actually, it is a free rendition of Psalm text frequently quoted.

[5]   Romans 2, 14 and 3, 27.

must die." Furthermore, Moses has handed down a Law of Good Works in Exodus 20, 13, and in Deuteronomy 5,17: "You shall not kill"; and "whoever strikes a man a mortal blow must be put to death" (Exodus 21,12). "You shall not commit adultery" (Exodus 20,14). "If a man commits adultery with his neighbor's wife, he shall be put to death" (Leviticus 20,10; cf. John 8,5). But what says the law of faith, which commands us to love our enemies,[6] and to carry our daily cross,[7] and to value our life but little?[8] "Do not be afraid, little flock, for it pleased your father to give you the kingdom" (Luke 12,32, Matth. 5,3). In John 16,33: "Take courage, I have overcome the world." And in Matthew 28,20: "Behold, I am with you all days, even unto the consummation of the world." This law the Apostles illustrated when they themselves departed cheerfully from the Sanhedrin, though having just been scourged for the sake of the name of Jesus.[9] Thus Paul in his Philippians 4,13 asserts: "I can do all things in him who strengthens me."

All this is contained in Ecclesiasticus 15,15: "He added his commandments and precepts." To whom? In the beginning he personally transmitted them to the first two humans. Later to the Jewish people through Moses and the prophets. The law announced the will of God. It placed sanctions on disobedience, and it promised reward to obedient man. Otherwise God through creation allows to their will the power of choice which he gave free and moveable in both directions. Therefore, "if thou wilt keep the commandments and offer acceptable fidelity forever, they shall preserve thee," and again "stretch forth thy hand to which thou wilt" (Ecclesiasticus 15,16-17). If the differences of good and evil and the will of God had remained hidden from man, the wrong choice could not be imputed to man. Had the will not been free, sin could not be at-

[6] Matthew 5, 44.
[7] Luke 9, 23.
[8] Matthew 10, 39, Luke 14, 26, John 12, 25 and 1 John 2, 15.
[9] Acts 5, 40 f.

tributed to man, since it ceases to be sin if it is not voluntary, the only exception being when error or obligation
arises out of [deliberate] sin. It is clear that a woman is
not to blame for being ravished.

Although this quotation from Ecclesiasticus applies especially to our first parents, it is in a certain sense valid for
Adam's entire progeny. But how could it concern us, if
there were no faculty of free will in us? Although the free
will has been wounded through sin, it is not extinct; though
it has contracted a paralysis, making us before the reception
of grace more readily inclined towards evil than good, free
will has not been destroyed. Only to the extent that monstrous crimes or the habit of sin, having become our second
nature, dim at times the judgment of our intellect and bury
thereby the free will, does the former seem destroyed and
the latter dead.

18) *Freedom and Grace according to Pelagius and Duns Scotus*

Views concerning the capacity of our free will after the
Fall of Man and before the reception of grace differ aston-
ishingly among ancient and modern thinkers, with one or
the other aspect being emphasized. Whoever wanted to
counter despair or a false sense of security, and thereby
spur man to hope and aspiration, has actually overrated the
freedom of the will.

Pelagius taught that no new grace was needed once grace
had liberated and healed the free will of man. Thus the
free will by itself was deemed sufficient to achieve eternal
salvation. But we owe salvation solely to God without whose
grace the will of man could not be effectively free to achieve
good. The strength of soul, with which man can pursue the
good he knows and avoid all evil, is in itself a gift of the
creator who could have made a frog instead of man.

Whoever agrees with Duns Scotus,[10] is more favorable

---

[10] Cf. chapter II, footnote 1. Duns Scotus, known also as Doctor
subtilis, became founder of Scotism, traditional philosophy of the

to the freedom of the will, whose power they believe to be so great that inasmuch as a man has not received redeeming grace, could nevertheless by his natural powers perform good works, by which he could properly, though not deservedly, merit sanctifying grace.[11] For these are the terms they employ.

19) Freedom and Grace according to St. Augustine and the Reformers

Diametrically opposed is the view that all morally good deeds [without grace] are detestable in God's sight no less than criminal deeds such as murder and adultery, because they do not originate in faith nor in love of God. This judgment is obviously too severe. The fact remains that there have been philosophers who possessed some knowledge of God, and hence perhaps also some trust and love

---

Franciscan Order, and differing in some respects from Thomism. Free will he held as the immediate cause of its volition. God has no immediate efficacy. Without free will there would be no possibility to sin. During the Renaissance Scotists opposed the classical revival. Most of the Scotist philosophy and theory has been relegated to the background today.

[11] Erasmus' discussion of grace suffers from obscurities. He was not well disposed to any scholastic terminology and failed to define clearly his own definitions. He does not enter into the controversy on the nature of sufficient and efficacious grace. He merely stresses the patristic argument that grace is necessary. Owing to its gratuitous character, grace cannot be earned by strictly natural merits, either in strict justice (meritum de condigno), i.e., according to worthiness, or as a matter of fitness (meritum de congruo), i.e., according to equity. Erasmus also uses the terms gratia gratum faciens (ingratiating grace) for sanctifying grace and gratia peculiaris for extraordinary grace. Joined to free will these terms can be reduced to gratia praeveniens et cooperans. A prevenient (operative) grace is an antecedent act of the soul. A subsequent (cooperating) grace usually presupposes a deliberate act of the will. All these graces "help man to perform salutary acts" (ad salutem). See especially Section 20 on the four varieties of grace in Erasmus' own words. For an orthodox survey see articles on "Grace" by J. Pohle, The Catholic Encyclopedia, New York, 1909, Volume VI, pp. 689-714.

of God, and did not act solely out of vainglory's sake, but rather out of love of virtue and goodness, which, they taught, was to be loved for no other reason but that it is good. For, whether a man who risks death for his country out of vainglory performs a morally good act in the general concrete or in the morally abstract, I do not know.

St. Augustine and his followers give a greater stress to the role of grace, as Paul also affirms it at every opportunity, because they are all conscious of how it debases true piety if man relies solely on his own strength. Thus Augustine challenges the view that man, subject to sin, can better himself or act to save himself. Only undeserved divine grace can spur man supernaturally to wish that which will lead to eternal life. This is known to some as prevenient grace. Augustine calls it operative grace. For him faith, through which we enter eternity, is also a free gift of God. So is charity an additional gift of the Spirit. Augustine calls it cooperative grace. It assists those who strive until they have reached their goal. Although free will and grace together accomplish the same work, grace is the leading cause and not just a concomitant one. But some are divided even on this opinion and say: if one considers the act according to its nature, then the will of man is the more important cause; if one considers, however, the meritorious aspects of the act, then grace is the more important.

Now, it appears that faith which evinces our desire to do salutary things, and charity which wishes us not to be frustrated in our desire, are not distinct in time, as they are different in their nature. Both can however be intensified in time.

20) *Four Varieties of Grace*

Since grace means a freely given gift, we may enumerate three or four varieties of grace.

The first kind of grace we possess by nature. Sin has

corrupted, but not extinguished it, as we said before, and some call it the natural influence. Even the most obstinate sinner will retain this grace which is common to all mankind. Thus, everyone is free to speak or to keep silent, to sit or to stand up, to help the poor, to read holy books, to listen to sermons. Some now hold that such acts in themselves can in no way lead to eternal life. Others assert that such works, because of God's immense goodness can prepare for the reception of grace, and can move God to be merciful. True, some deny that this can happen without special grace. Therefore, this first kind of grace, common to all, is seldom called grace. Yet, it actually is such. For God as creator, conservor and governor of this world every day achieves greater miracles than the healing of a leper or the exorcism of demons. But we don't call these divine acts of maintaining the world miracles, because they are obvious to us every day.

A second variety is extraordinary grace. God through mercy moves the undeserving sinner to contrition. But God does not yet infuse that ultimate grace which can eliminate his sin and make him once more pleasing to Himself. Thus a sinner aided by this second kind of grace, which we had called operative, is displeased with himself. Yet, though he has not abandoned the inclination to sin, he is capable of giving alms, can pray, practice pious exercises, listen to sermons, request pious people to intercede for him with God, and thus by means of these and other ethically good works, apply in a way for obtaining the ultimate grace.

The goodness of God does not refuse to any mortals this second grace. The mercy of God offers everyone favorable opportunities for repentance. One needs only to attach the rest of one's own will to God's help, which merely invites to, but does not compel to betterment. Furthermore, one finds the opinion, that it is within our power to turn our will towards or away from grace—just as it is our pleasure to open or close our eyes against light. It is incompatible with the infinite love of God for man that a man's striving with all his might for grace should be frustrated. Through that grace, which they call sanctifying, if he inspires to it with all his power, it results that no sinner should be overconfident, none again should despair. No one perishes except through his own fault.

There are then first natural grace, second an exciting or operative grace, which is, to be sure, imperfect, third an efficient grace, which we have called cooperative, and which promotes that which is begun, and fourth a grace which leads to the final goal. The last three are supposedly one and the same grace, even though according to its operation in us, we call it by different names. Thus, the first excites, the second promotes and the third leads to the goal.

21) *Views of Thomists, Carlstadt, and Luther*

There are then those who are quite removed from Pelagius in ascribing more to grace and hardly anything to the free will, though not completely abolishing it. They deny that man could desire anything good without extraordinary grace, that he can initiate, continue and reach the goal without the guiding and continuous help of divine grace. Such an opinion appears quite probable, because it leaves man the possibility of exerting himself and striving, and nevertheless relinquishing to him nothing which he could solely ascribe to his own powers.[12]

But more objectionable is the opinion of those who emphatically affirm that the will in itself can only commit sin and that only grace can cause good; and this grace operates not through or with the will but merely within the will; in such wise that the will is in this case like wax in the hands of the sculptor; that it takes on any form pleasing to the craftsman.[13] These people, I think, have so

---

[12] Appears an oversimplification of the Thomistic position.
[13] Sketch of Carlstadt's view.

great a fear of and distrust of meritorious human acts that they go too far.[14]

Yet, worst of all is obviously the opinion of those who maintain that the free will is an empty name and that neither among the angels, nor Adam, nor us, nor before or after receiving grace did it or could it accomplish anything;[15] that rather God causes in us evil as well as good, and that everything happens of mere necessity.

22) *A Textual Criticism of Ecclesiasticus*

Hence I shall discuss these latter two opinions. In all this I have been somewhat lengthy to make it easier for the lay reader to understand the remaining argumentation —I am writing as a layman for laymen. At first I have quoted *Ecclesiasticus* [15, 14-18] which seems best to demonstrate the origin and power of the free will. Now we shall peruse somewhat more quickly the remaining scriptural evidence.

But first we must take note of the fact that the Aldine edition[16] has a different text from the Latin one used in the Church. "They shall preserve thee"[17] is missing in the Greek manuscripts. Even Augustine, although quoting this text a number of times, does not add these words either. Probably one ought to read ποιῆται instead of ποιῆσαι.[18]

---

[14] "Ut praeter casam" refers to a proverb of Terence (195?-159 *BC*), *Phormio* 768, Roman writer of comedies, "ita fugias, ne praeter casam," i.e., when in flight avoid your own house. It means in Erasmus "to go too far."

[15] Luther's view.

[16] Aldina refers to a Venetian printing (1518) of the Greek text.

[17] Ecclesiasticus 15, 16.

[18] One must recall that Erasmus had worked on the Greek version of the Bible. This was not only an important development in Biblical textual criticism, but also a great help to Luther's Bible translation. Present higher criticism considers this example by Erasmus a bit pedantic. Cf. the Greek text of Ecclesiasticus 15, 15: ". . . and to perform its faithfulness, will be of thine own good pleasure."

23) *Additional Old Testament Proofs*

Now God has offered already in paradise the choice between life and death. If you obey my laws you shall live; if you disobey, you must die; beware of evil and choose the good. In the same vein he spoke to Cain: "Why are you angry and why are you downcast? If you do well, will you not be accepted; but if you do not well, will not sin crouch at the door? Its desire is for you, but you must master it" (Genesis 4,6-7). Here reward is in prospect for whoever chooses the good, and punishment for whoever prefers evil. Simultaneously this passage shows that bad inclinations can be overcome and that they don't necessitate sinning. With this passage agrees also the Lord's saying to Moses: "I have set before you life and death. Choose the good and follow me."[19] Could it be stated any more plainly? God shows what is good and what is evil. He offers as recompense death or life. He relinquishes to man the freedom of choice. It would be ridiculous to command one to make a choice, if he were incapable of turning in either direction. That's like saying to someone who stands at the crossroads "choose either one," when only one is passable. Again in Deuteronomy 30,15-19:

> *Here, then, I have today set before you life and prosperity, death and doom. If you obey the commandments of the Lord, Your God, which I enjoin on you today, loving him, and walking in his ways, and keeping his commandments, statutes and decrees, you will live and grow numerous, and the Lord, your God, will bless you in the land you are entering to occupy. If, however, you turn away your hearts and will not listen, but are led astray and adore and serve other gods, I tell you now that you will certainly perish; you will not have a long life on the land which you are crossing the Jordan to enter and occupy. I call heaven and earth today to witness against you: I have set before you life and death, the blessing and the curse. Choose life, then, that you and your descendants may live.*

---

[19]   This appears to be a free rendition of Deuteronomy 30, 19.

You hear again and again of preparing, choosing, preventing, meaningless words, if the will of man were not also free to do good, and not just evil. Otherwise it would be like addressing a man whose hands are tied in such a manner that he can reach with them only to the left, "To your right is excellent wine, to your left you have poison. Take what you like."

The above agrees also with what the Lord says in Isaiah: "If you be willing and harken to me, you shall eat the good things of the land. But if you will not, and will provoke me to wrath, the sword shall devour you" (Isaiah 1,19). Assuming man has no will to do good, or even, as some assert, neither good nor evil, what is the meaning then of "if you be willing" and "if you will not"? It would be more fitting [for God] to say, "if I will" and "if I will not." Since the above is often said to sinners, I do not see how one can avoid attributing to them also a free will capable of choosing the good, because the will presumes certitude and discernment—unless, of course, one prefers to speak only of an emotion or a rationalization.

Furthermore, in the same prophet we read: "If you seek, seek; return, come" (Isaiah 21,12). What is the use of urging people to return and to come, if they are quite unable to do so? Is it not like telling one bound in chains, whom you do not want to untie, "get up, come and follow me"? Also : "Assemble yourselves and come, and draw near together" (Isaiah 45, 20), and "Be converted to me, and you shall be saved" (Isaiah 45, 22). Again: "Arise, arise . . . shake yourself from the dust. . . . loose the bonds from off thy neck" (Isaiah 52, 1-2). The same in Jeremiah 15, 19: "If thou wilt be converted, I will convert thee . . . and if thou shalt separate the precious from the vile, thou shalt be as my mouth." Free choice is implied in "if thou shalt separate."

Zachariah indicates even clearer the effort of the free will: "Turn ye to me, saith the Lord, and I will turn you, saith the Lord of hosts" (Zachariah 1,3). And the Lord says: "If the wicked one do penance for all his sins which he hath committed, and do justice and judgment. . . I will not remember all his iniquities that he hath done" (Ezekiel 18, 21), as well as, "But if the just man turn himself away from his justice, and do iniquity. . ." (Ezekiel 18,24). In this chapter the words "turn away, do commit" are often repeated, both in an evil and a good sense. But where are those who say that man does nothing, but endures everything through operative grace? In Ezekiel 18,31: "Cast away from you all your transgressions," and "Why will you die, O house of Israel?" And in Ezekiel 33,11: "I desire not the death of the wicked . . . turn ye . . . and come." Would a pious God deplore the death of his people, which he himself is causing? If he does not wish our death, we must impute it to our own will, if we perish. Certainly nothing can be imputed to one unable to do good or evil. That mystic psalmist would be exhorting in vain people not in control of their will: "Turn away from evil and do good, seek after peace and pursue it."[20]

But how little is accomplished by quoting selections of this sort. The entire Holy Scripture is filled with such exhortations. In Joel 2,12: "Be converted to me with all your heart." In Jonah 3,8: "Let them turn everyone from his evil way." In Isaiah 46,8: "Return, ye transgressors, to the heart." "And be converted everyone from his evil way, that I may repent me of the evil that I think to do unto them for the wickedness of their doings" (Jeremiah 26,3), and "If you will not hearken to me to walk in my law" (Jeremiah 26,4). Scripture desires nothing but conversion, ardor, and improvement. All these exhortations would lose their meaning if really necessity were to determine good or evil acts. Just as senseless would be the many promises, threats, remonstrances, reproaches, entreaties, blessings and maledictions, addressed to willing and unwilling ears, as the following: "I see how stiffnecked this people is" (Exodus 32,9); "O my people, what have I done to thee" (Micheas 6,3); "They cast away my statutes"

---

[20] In the text Erasmus refers to Psalms 36 which, however, contains no such passage. He may actually have had Psalm 33, 15 in mind, which David sang feigning madness before Abimelech.

(Ezekiel 20,13); "O that my people would hearken to me, that Israel would walk in my ways" (Psalm 80,14); "Who is the man . . . that he may see good? Then guard thy tongue from evil" (Psalm 33, 13-14).

Furthermore, whenever the word "will" is used, it implies free will. Doesn't the reader of such passages ask: why do you [God] make conditional promises, when it depends solely on your will? Why do you blame me, when all my works, good or bad, are accomplished by you, and I am only your tool? Why blame me, when it is neither in my power to preserve what you gave me, nor to keep away the evil you implant in me? Why do you implore me, when everything depends on you anyhow and can be carried out only by your will? Why bless me, as if I had done my duty, when everything is your achievement? Why do you curse me, when I have merely sinned through necessity? What is the purpose of all the many commandments, if it is impossible for anybody to keep them? Of course, there are those who deny that man, as much as he may be justified by faith and charity, can fulfill God's commandments. They insist that all good works, because done according to the "flesh," must lead to damnation, unless a merciful God, for the sake of their faith, pardons them.

But again the Lord's words spoken through Moses in Deuteronomy 30, 11-14 are plain. The fulfillment of the commandment is not only possible for us, but even easy.

> For this command which I enjoin on you today is not too mysterious and remote for you. It is not up in the sky, that you should say, "Who will go up in the sky to get it for us and tell us of it, that we may carry it out?" Nor is it across the sea, that you should say, "Who will cross the sea to get it for us and tell us of it, that we may carry it out?" No, it is something very near to you, already in your mouths and in your hearts; you have only to carry it out.

This quotation concerns the greatest of all the commandments, to turn to the Lord your God with all your heart and your whole soul. Or what does it mean to hear, to obey, to turn, if it is not within your power?

I don't want to take any further pains and collect such

quotations, since Scripture abounds in them. It is like looking for water in the ocean. Consequently, as already stated, a large part of Scripture would obviously be ineffectual if one accepts the last two of the above-mentioned three opinions [against the freedom of the will].[21]

Finally, there are several places in Scripture which obviously ascribe contingency to God, yes, even a certain mutability. For example in Jeremias 18,8 and 10:

> *If that nation against which I have spoken, shall repent of their evil, I also will repent of the evil that I have thought to do to them . . . If it shall do evil in my sight, that it obey not my voice, I will repent of the goal that I have spoken to do unto it.*

Now we know very well that Scripture in this instance, as in many others, speaks in human terms. God is not confused by mutability. Actually, one only says of God that he has abandoned his anger and has become merciful after we have bettered ourselves and he deigns us worthy of his grace; conversely, that he has deprived us of grace and has become angry whenever we have changed for the worse and he punishes and humbles us.

The prophet Isaias spoke to Ezechias in 4 Kings 20,1: "Thou shalt die and not live." But soon after much weeping the same prophet assures with his message: "I have heard thy prayer, and I have seen thy tears, and behold I have healed thee," etc. And again in 2 Kings 12,10 Nathan tells David: "The sword shall never depart from thy house" etc. But no sooner has David said: "I have sinned against the Lord," Nathan says to David: "The Lord also hath taken away thy sin; thou shalt not die." As in these, so in other passages, it is improper to think of a changeable God. Yet, we cannot but realize that there dwells a flexible will in us. If necessity guides it towards evil, how can sin be attributed to it? Or if it is guided by necessity towards good, why does God change from anger to mercy, since we deserve also in this case no requital?

---

[21]   Meaning the views of Carlstadt and Luther. Cf. Section 21.

IV

NEW TESTAMENT PROOFS
SUPPORTING THE FREE WILL

THUS far the discussion has centered on proofs taken from the Old Testament. Some people could dispute these, had they not all been of the kind of those that were not abolished but received more probatory strength through the Gospels. Let us therefore turn to the books of the New Testament.

In the New Testament we meet first of all the place where Christ weeps over the destruction of Jerusalem.[1]

> *Jerusalem, Jerusalem! Thou who killest the prophets, and stonest those who are sent to thee! How often would I have gathered thy children together, as a hen gathers her young under her wings, but thou wouldst not!*

If all had happened merely through necessity, could Jerusalem not have been justified in answering the weeping Lord, "Why do you torment yourself with useless weeping? If it was your will that we should not listen to the prophets, why did you send them? Why do you blame us for what you willed, while we have acted merely out of necessity? You wished to collect us, but you did not will this within us, rather caused us not to wish it." [In reality,] however, the words of the Lord do not blame a necessity in the Jews, but rather their wicked and obstinate will: I wanted to gather you, but you did not want it.

---

[1] Matthew 23, 37.

24) *Commandments and Exhortations; Reward and Punishment*

Again: "If thou wilt enter into life, keep the commandments" (Matth. 19,17). How could one ask somebody "if thou wilt be perfect, go, sell what thou hast" (Matth. 19,21). "If anyone wishes to come after me, let him deny himself, and take up his cross daily, and follow me" (Luke 9,23). Although this is a very difficult commandment, nevertheless the appeal is to the will. Subsequently, "For he who would save his life will lose it" (Luke 9,24). Wouldn't even the clearest commandment of Christ be senseless, if we could expect nothing from the human will? "Amen, amen I say to you" and again "Amen I say to you" (Matth. 5,22 and 28). "If you love me, keep my commandments" (John 14,15). How often does John alone impress this upon us! The word "if" does not at all imply necessity, as, for example, "If you abide in me, and if my words abide in you" (John 15,7), as well as, "If thou wilt be perfect" (Matth. 19,21).

When Scripture talks of good and bad works, as well as of reward, I don't understand how necessity fits in. Neither nature, nor necessity can earn merit. Our Lord Jesus says moreover, "Rejoice and exult, because your reward is great in heaven" (Matth. 5,12).

What does the parable of the laborers in the vineyard tell us? Are there workers who don't work? Each one received contractually one denarius as a kind of remuneration for his work. One hears this objection: a reward is something God owes us, because he has pledged his will to us, in case we believe in his promise. However, faith itself is a work and the free will participates to a considerable measure in it by turning to or away from faith. Why was the servant praised who had increased the fortune of his master by his diligence, and why was the idle one damned, if man in such a case was not responsible?[2] And

---

[2]   Matthew 25, 14-30.

again in Matthew 25,35 Christ mentions not necessity, but the good works of men, when he invites all to participate in his eternal kingdom. You gave me to eat, you gave me to drink, you took me in, you clothed me and so on. Again those on his left hand he does not reproach with necessity, but with the willing omission of works: you have seen me hungry, here was an opportunity for a good work, but you did not give me to eat, etc.

The entire Gospel is filled with exhortations. "Come to me, all you who labor and are burdened" (Matth. 11,28), "watch" (Matth. 24,42), "pray" (Matth. 5,44), "ask . . . seek . . . knock" (Matth. 7,7). "take heed . . . beware" (Mark 8,15). What is the meaning of these many parables concerning the word of God which "we should preserve" (Matth. 13,1-8)? Concerning the bridegroom whom we should hasten to meet (Matth. 25,1-13); concerning the thief coming at night, digging for treasures (Matth. 24,43; 1 Thessalonians 5,2); concerning the house which must be built on rock (Matth. 7,24). Of course, these parables are to spur us to exertion, diligence and zeal, and not to our ruin by being indifferent towards the grace of God. These words would be superfluous and powerless, if everything could be reduced to necessity.

The same can be said of evangelical threats: "But woe to you, Scribes and Pharisees, hypocrites" (Matth. 23,13), "Woe to the Corozaim!" (Matth. 11,21). Futile would also be reproaches like, "O unbelieving generation, how long shall I be with you? How long shall I put up with you?" (Mark 9,18). "Serpents, brood of vipers, how are you to escape the judgment of hell?" (Matth. 23,33). The Lord speaks, "Therefore, by their fruits you will know them" (Matth. 7,20). "Fruits" mean to him works, and these he designated to be ours. But they could not be ours, if all happened of necessity. He prays on the cross, "Father, forgive them, for they do not know what they are doing" (Luke 23,34). How much correcter would it have been to justify them, that they had no free will, and were incapable of acting differently, even if they had wished to do so.

Again John says, "He gave the power of becoming sons of God to those believing in his name" (John 1,12). How could power to become children of God be given to those who are not yet sons of God, if there is no freedom of the will? When some had taken offense at the words of the master and had fallen away from him, he said to his disciples: "Do you also wish to go away?" (John 6,68). Had the former fallen away out of necessity rather than their own impulse, why did he ask the others, whether they too were going to leave him?

But we don't want to bore the reader with the enumeration of all such passages. They exist in such profusion that they occur easily to everyone by themselves.

25) *God's Judgment*

Now we want to investigate whether also in Paul, the zealous advocate of grace, who storms the works of [the Jewish] laws, we find something which implies the freedom of the will. Thus we meet above all a passage in the Epistle to the Romans: "Dost thou despise the riches of his goodness and patience and long-suffering? Dost thou not know that the greatness of God is meant to lead thee to repentance?" (Romans 2,4). How could the disdain of a commandment be imputed, if there is no free will? And how could God invite us to do penance, when he has caused impenitence? And how could a condemnation be justified, when the judge himself has compelled the [committing of an] outrage? But Paul had just finished saying, "and we know that the judgment of God is according to truth against those who do such things" (Romans 2,2). Here he speaks of "doing," and of a judgment according to truth. Where is mere necessity? Where is the will that merely suffers? Mark well whom Paul does blame for evil: "But according to thy hardness and unrepented heart, thou dost treasure up to thyself wrath in the day of wrath, and of the revelation of the just judgment of God who will render to every man according to his works" (Romans

2,5). The reference here is to a just judgment of God and to works which deserve punishment. If God ascribes to us only his own good works which he performs through us, and we thus earn glory, honor and immortality, then his goodness appears plausible. Although even in such a case the Apostle adds, "life eternal indeed he will give to those who by patience in good works seek glory and honor and immortality" (Romans 2,7). But how could it be justified that "wrath and indignation . . . tribulation and anguish" (Romans 12,8-9) shall be visited upon the transgressor, if he is doing nothing freely, but everything through necessity?

26) *Running the Race*

Would not already the Pauline parable of the runner, the prize and the crown of victory be untenable, if nothing were attributed to our striving? In 1 Corinthians 9,24 we read: "Do you not know that those who run in a race, all indeed run, but one receives the prize? So run as to obtain it." And [he adds], "they [run] indeed to receive a perishable crown, but we an imperishable one." A prize can only be won by somebody who has fought. Only one who had earned it can receive it as a presentation. Furthermore: "Fight the good fight of the faith, lay hold on the life eternal" (1 Timothy 6,12). Wherever a competition takes place, we are dealing with a voluntary striving, and there exists the danger that a relaxation in endeavor will deprive one of the prize. This is completely different where everything happens through necessity. Also: "And again, one who enters a contest is not crowned unless he has competed according to the rules" (2 Timothy 2,5). And [two verses] before: "Conduct thyself in work as a good soldier of Christ Jesus" (2 Timothy 2,3). The industrious husbandman is mentioned (2 Timothy 2,6). The competitor obtains a prize, the soldier his reward, the countryman his harvest. The same: "I have fought the good fight, I have finished the course, . . . For the rest, there is laid up for me a crown of justice, which the Lord, the just Judge, will give me in that day" (2 Timothy 4,7). Such words as fight, crown, just judge, to give, to fight,—to me—seem difficult to be reconciled with mere necessity, whereby the will does absolutely nothing but endure.

27) *Warding off the Works of Darkness*

But also[the Apostle] James attributed human sin not to necessity, nor to a God operating within us, but to depraved concupiscence. "Let no man say when he is tempted, that he is tempted by God. . . But everyone is tempted by his own passion. Then when passion has conceived, it brings forth sin" (James 1,13-15).

The sins of man, Paul calls "the works of the flesh," and not the works of God.[3] He obviously designates as "flesh" what James calls concupiscence. In the Acts of the Apostles this question is put to Ananias: "Why has Satan tempted thy heart?" (Acts 5,3). Paul, too, attributes evil deeds to the spirits of the air about us who work on the unbelievers.[4] "What harmony is there between Christ and Belial?" (2 Corinthians 6,15). "Either make the tree good and its fruits good, or make the tree bad and its fruits bad" (Matth. 12,33). How can some people dare to ascribe to an unsurpassably good God the worst of fruits? Although Satan can entice human concupiscence by external means, or also by internal ones, rooted in human circumstances, the enticement itself does not necessitate sinning, as long as we want to combat it and implore divine aid. Just the same, when the Spirit of Christ excites us to good deeds, it does not constitute a compulsion, but rather an aid. With James agrees also Ecclesiasticus 15,21: "He hath commanded no man to do wickedly, and he hath given no man license to sin." Now, compulsion is even more than a commandment. Even clearer is what Paul writes: "If anyone, therefore, has cleansed himself from these, he will be a vessel for honorable use" (2 Timothy 2,1). How

---

[3]   Galatians 5, 19.
[4]   Ephesians 2, 2.

could someone keep clean, if he is totally incapable of doing anything?

I know that this is a mode of figurative expression. For the moment I am quite satisfied that it contradicts those who want to ascribe everything to mere necessity. The same mode of expression is found in 1 John 3,3: "And everyone who has this hope in Him makes himself holy, just as He is holy." I again admit to my opponents that this is a mode of expression. They also must permit us to employ occasionally figurative usage of words. But it is impudent for them to interpret "he makes himself holy" to mean "he is made holy by God, whether he likes it or not."

"Let us lay aside the works of darkness" (Romans 13,12), "Strip off the old man with his deeds" (Colossians 3,9), exclaims Paul. How can we be commanded to lay aside something, if we are incapable? The same: "To wish is within my power, but I do not find the strength to accomplish what is good" (Romans 7,18). Paul obviously admits here that it is in the power of man to want to do good.

28) *Virtuous Endeavors Unite with Divine Grace*

Now the will to do good works is in itself a good work. Otherwise an evil will could not be something bad. Nobody denies that already the will to kill is something evil. And again, "The spirits of the prophets are under the control of the prophets" (1 Corinthians 14,32). Whoever is driven by the Holy Spirit is influenced by it, yet is also free to keep silent about it. How much freer is the volition of man! Those, to be sure, who are driven by a fanatical spirit can not keep quiet, even if they wanted to, and often don't understand themselves what they are saying.

Here belongs also the passage admonishing Timothy: "Do not neglect the grace granted thee" (1 Timothy 4,14). This declares that it is in our power to turn away from offered grace. The same in another passage: "His grace in me has not been fruitless" (1 Corinthians 15,10). The Apostle informs us that he has not left unused divine grace.

How could he assert this, if he had done nothing? "Do you according to your part strive diligently to supply your faith with virtue" (2 Peter 1,5), and so on. And a little further on: "Therefore, brethren, strive even more by good works to make your calling and election sure!" (2 Peter 1,10). Here the Apostle wants our virtuous endeavors to unite with divine grace, in order to reach perfection gradually through righteous deeds.

But I fear it could seem to some that this is an immoderate heaping together of passages encountered everywhere in Scripture. When Paul writes: "All Scripture is inspired by God and useful for teaching, for reproaching, for converting, for instructing in justice. . ." (2 Timothy 3, 16), there would obviously be no room for all this, if everything happened on account of pure and unavoidable necessity. What purpose would the many eulogies about pious men in Ecclesiasticus 44 serve, if human zeal deserved nothing? What's the meaning of obedience, praised everywhere, if man in his good as well as evil works is just a tool of God's, like the hatchet for the carpenter?

29) *Luther's Assertion*

We all would be such tools, if the teachings of Wycliffe were true. Accordingly, everything happens on account of pure necessity, be it before or after the reception of grace; may they be good, evil or ethically indifferent works. Luther agrees with this. In order to forestall anybody accusing me of inventing this, let me quote his own words taken from his *Assertio*.[5]

> *This article must be revoked. I have expressed it improperly, when I said that the free will, before obtaining grace, is really an empty name. I should have said straightforwardly that the free will is really a fiction and a label*

[5] Luther burned the Papal Bull, *Exsurge Domine*, condemning 42 of his propositions as heretical (June 15, 1520), and wrote in answer the *Assertio*. See chapter I, footnote 3. Erasmus wrote much of his *Diatribe* against this Article 36 of the *Assertio*.

without reality, because it is in no man's power to plan any evil or good. As the article of Wycliffe, condemned at Constance, correctly teaches: everything takes place by absolute necessity.

I have deliberately omitted many passages from the Acts [of the Apostles] and the Apocalypse [of St. John], otherwise I might be boring the reader. Suffice it to say that many passages have, not without reason, induced intelligent and pious men not to abandon free will completely. [In conclusion] it is not at all true that those who trust in their own works are driven by the spirit of Satan and delivered to damnation.

V

APPARENT PROOFS AGAINST
THE FREE WILL

IT IS now time to consider from another angle some scriptural testimony that seems completely to contradict the freedom of the will. Such we meet, of course, here and there in Holy Scripture. However, two passages are especially important and more obvious than the others, and both are dealt with by the Apostle Paul in such a manner that at first one has the impression he thinks nothing at all of human works and of the capacity of the free will.

30) *First Scriptural Passage: Pharaoh's Hardened Heart*

One passage is Exodus 9,12 and 16 which Paul treats in Romans 9,14:

> *But the Lord made Pharaoh obstinate, and he would not listen to the laws of God . . . But this is why I have spared you: to show you my power and to make my name resound throughout the earth.*

And Paul explains this by quoting a similar passage from Exodus 33,19 in his Epistle to the Romans:

> *For he says to Moses, "I will have mercy on whom I have mercy, and I will show pity to whom I will show pity."*
> *So then there is the question not of him who wills nor of him who runs, but of God showing mercy.*

The second passage is from Malachi 1,2 and is treated by Paul in Romans 9,11-13.

Was not Esau brother to Jacob, saith the Lord, and I have loved Jacob, but have hated Esau.

Paul explains it thus:

Before the children had yet been born, or had done aught of good or evil, in order that the selective purpose of God might stand, depending not on deeds, but on him who calls, it was said to her [Rebecca], "the older shall serve the younger," as it was written " 'Jacob I have loved, but Esau I have hated."

Since it is obviously contradictory that God, who is not only just, but also merciful, should have hardened the heart of a man, in order to show his might by the former's evilness, Origen resolves the difficulty in the third book of his *Commentary on St. John*[1] as follows: God permitted an occasion of induration, but the guilt is Pharaoh's. His malice caused him to become more obstinate, rather than penitential. Just as after the same rain well-tended land produces the best fruit, neglected land however thorns and thistles; just as wax becomes soft and clay hard under the same sun, so God's gentleness, tolerating a sinner, causes a change of mind in one and a hardening in evil in another. God shows mercy to him who remembers his goodness and betters himself. However, he hardens him who remembers his goodness and betters himself. However, he hardens him who, though obtaining a respite for a change of mind, does not care for God's goodness and becomes worse. [Origen] presents a figurative expression, customary in popular sermons, marking such a one as culprit who gives occasion for a [bad] deed, [as for example] when a father would say to his son that he has ruined him, because the former had not punished the latter immediately for a certain offense.

---

[1]   See Book 3, ch. I, 10 of περὶἀρχῶν, the Greek actually quoted in Erasmus text. See also chapter II, footnote E.

31) *Man Wills Evil*

Isaias employs a similar mode of expression: "Why hast thou made us to err, O Lord, from thy ways? Why hast thou hardened our heart, that we should not fear thee?" (Isaias 63,17). According to Origen this passage Jerome interprets to mean: God hardens a sinner, when he does not castigate him, and he pities a sinner, when he summons him to do penance, by means of afflictions. Thus the Lord exclaims angrily in Osee 4,14: "I will not visit upon your daughters when they shall commit fornication." On the other hand, he punishes out of pity when he speaks: "I will punish their crimes with a rod, and their sin with stripes" (Psalms 88,33).

Jeremias uses the same mode of expression: "Thou hast deceived me, O Lord, and I am deceived: thou hast been stronger than I, and thou hast prevailed" (Jeremias 20,7). A deceiver is here meant to be someone who does not restrain one from an aberration. Origen considers such attitude more conducive to a perfect healing, just as the experienced surgeon values a slow healing of a wound, permitting the pus to exude more readily. The result is a more lasting cure. Origen also notices that the Lord said: "But this is why I have spared you" (Exodus 9,16), rather than "created you." Otherwise the Pharaoh could not be called godless, since "God saw that all he had made was very good" (Genesis 1,31). In reality Pharaoh was created with a will enabling him to move in both directions. He has turned evil on his own account, since he preferred to follow his own inclination, rather than obey God's commandments.

32) *God Uses Free Will*

This malice of Pharaoh God has utilized for his honor and for the salvation of his people; thus revealing even better that it is vain of man to oppose the will of God. In the same manner a clever king or a "pater familias" will use the hardness of men, however odious it may be to him, in order to punish villains. Nevertheless, the free will is not violated when the outcome of an event is in God's hands, and when God according to his hidden decision guides men differently from what they have resolved. Just as he guides the intentions of the villains to benefit the pious, so the intentions of the latter miss their goal if God's grace does not assist them. This is what Paul means when he says: "So then there is question not of him who wills nor of him who runs, but of God showing mercy" (Romans 9,16). God's mercy precedes our will, accompanies it, and gives it fruitfulness. Nevertheless it remains that we wish, run and attain, except that all this we must ascribe to God, to whom we belong with everything we are.

33) *God's Foreknowledge*

The knotty point how God's foreknowledge is compatible with our free will has often been amplified. But in my opinion Lorenzo Valla[2] has been most successful at it: Foreknowledge does not cause what is to take place. Even we know many things which will be happening. They will not happen because we know them, but vice versa. An eclipse of the sun does not occur because astronomers predict it, but it can be predicted, precisely because it will take place.

34) *God's Predestination*

More difficult becomes the question when we consider God's will or determination, meaning that God wills that which He knows beforehand. Somehow He must wish the foreknown, seeing that He does not prevent it though he could do so. This is what Paul means when he comments: "For who resists his will?" (Romans 9,19). "He has mercy on whom he will, and whom he will he hardens" (Romans 9,18). Assuming a king could do, unopposed, as he pleases,

---

[2] This is the other of Erasmus' two references to Valla. Cf. ch. II, footnote 3.

then everything he wishes would be called his "doing."

Thus it might appear that God's will, which is the first cause of all that happens, seems to deprive us of the free will. Paul does not discuss this question, rather he scolds those who want to investigate it, "O man, who art thou to reply to God?" (Romans 9,20). However, he scolds the man who would impiously complain, just as a master might well say to his stubborn servant that he should not inquire after the why of a given order, but rather carry it out. The master's answer would be different if an understanding and willing servant desires modestly to know why the master wants something to be done which appears to be useless.

God had wanted the Pharaoh to perish miserably. He was justified in wishing this, and it was good that the tyrant did perish. The will of God, however, did not force him to persist in his wrong. Thus a master may give an order to a servant whose bad character he knows. Such an order may offer the opportunity for sin and, caught in it, his punishment may serve as a lesson to others. The master knows beforehand that the servant will sin, and thus display his real character; in a certain sense, he wills his destruction and his sin. Nonetheless, this does not excuse the servant, for he sins out of his own malice. He has deserved that his malice be known to all and be punished. But where could you assume the beginning of merit where there is eternal necessity and where there is no free will?

35) *Efficiency of the Good Will of Man*

When we were saying that God often permits an action to end differently than planned by men, it does not hold true in most cases, and it happens more frequently among evil than good people. The Jews crucified the Lord with the purpose of removing him completely. This wicked plan God turned to the honor of his son, and to the welfare of the entire world. That centurion Cornelius who competed for God's favor with good works, obtained what he wished for.[3] Paul, too, finished the race and won the victory crown for which he competed.[4]

36) *Primary and Secondary Causes*

I do not want to investigate here whether God, who is without any doubt the first and principal cause of all happenings, effects some things only through secondary causes, eliminating himself from those, or whether he is causing everything in the sense of the primary cause, with secondary causes only cooperating, but without necessity. It can certainly not be doubted that God, if he wants to, can deflect the natural effect of all secondary causes into its opposite. He could effect in a natural manner that something becomes cool and moist through fire, hard and dry through water, shaded by the sun, that streams will not run and rocks will flow, that poison becomes nourishment and food poison. Thus the three youths in the Babylonian furnace remained uninjured, while the Chaldeans were destroyed by its heat.[5] When God performs such, we speak of a miracle. In this way he can also deprive the palate of its taste, the eyes of their judgment, stupefy the powers of the intellect, memory and will. In this manner he compels men to do what he has decided. This he did with Balaam who came to curse and when he could not, was not responsible for what he was saying.[6] But such expectations should not be generalized. For even in these cases God wished everything for just reasons, which are, however, not always known to us. His will cannot be resisted. Yet, indisputably man often opposes this "ordained will," as the scholastics call it. Or did Jerusalem not oppose, when it refused to be gathered in, though this was God's will?[7]

---

[3] Acts 10.
[4] 2 Timothy 4, 7 f.
[5] Daniel 3, 19 ff.
[6] Cf. Numbers 23.
[7] Matthew 23, 37.

37) *Conditional and Unconditional Necessity*

But someone may object, saying that for two reasons necessity governs the results of an action: namely, neither can the foreknowledge of God be a delusion, nor his will be hindered. I answer: not every necessity excludes the freedom of the will. For example, God the Father necessarily generates the Son. At the same time He generates Him willingly, since He is not forced [from outside His nature] to do so.

In human life there can also be a necessity which does not yet exclude the freedom of the will. God knew beforehand, and because he did, he somehow wished that Judas would betray the Lord. If you consider God's infallible foreknowledge and his unchangeable will, Judas had to betray the Lord. Nevertheless, Judas could have changed his will. He certainly would not have had to give in to an evil one. But what if he had changed? Well, even then God's foreknowledge would not have been wrong and his will not hindered, because in such a case he would have known and willed that change also.

If one wants to discuss the matter with scholastic subtlety, one may assume in such cases a determination of the consequent act, but not of the actor.[8] These are the usual terms. Admittedly, Judas had to betray the Lord, if God wished this with his eternally effective will. But it is contested that he had to betray him for that reason, since he accomplished the evil deed rather on the strength of his own evil will.

---

[8] On predestination Erasmus is very elementary and orthodox. He does not enter into the problem of the "foreseen merits" of the just but merely states Valla's view that foreknowledge is not predetermination. Scholastic philosophy distinguishes antecedent necessity (*necessitas consequentis*) from consequent necessity (*necessitas consequentiae*). As God foresees the free acts of men, Erasmus argues, they are determined *not* by antecedent necessity, a necessity which would determine the free will of the agent, but by consequent necessity, the historical fact that, granted free choice, the act would inevitably take place.

It is not my purpose here to pursue such subtleties. What Exodus 7 has been saying about God's hardening the Pharaoh's heart could be accepted in the Pauline version: "God has given them up to a reprobate sense" (Romans 1,18), thus sin and punishment of sin coincide in this case. Whomever God abandons to a reprobate sense has deserved it, as Pharaoh did, who wished not to dismiss the Israelites, although he was warned by many signs; or like the philosophers who worship wood and stones, though knowing God's supernatural perfection. Wherever there is pure and perpetual necessity, there can be neither guilt nor virtue. One cannot deny that every human act is accompanied by a divine act, because every action is a reality, indeed a certain good, as for example to wish to or actually embrace an adulteress. The evil of an action does not proceed from God, but from our own will, except, as mentioned above, one might state that God is the cause of the evil of the human will only insofar as he leaves the will to itself and does not turn it aside by grace. It is just as one might say we ruin a man by not stopping his ruin, though we could do so. But this is enough concerning the first scriptural proof.

38) *Second Scriptural Passage: Jacob and Esau: Election and Rejection*

Now to the second, the one of Esau and Jacob, of whom was prophesied already before their birth: "The elder shall serve the younger" (Genesis 25,23).[9] This prophecy does not explicitly refer to the salvation of man. Without asking for his will, God can wish a man to be a servant or a pauper, and nevertheless not to be excluded from eternal salvation. When Paul adds the passage from Malachias 1,2: "I have loved Jacob but have hated Esau," one should not accept it literally, for God does not love the way we love, nor does he hate anyone. Such passions are not of God's essence. Moreover, what I really want to say, the prophet

---

[9] Cf. Erasmus, Section 30.

speaks in his passage obviously not of a hatred which damns man eternally, but of a temporal difficulty. It is the same when one speaks of God's anger and fury. The passage censured those who wished to rebuild Edom, though God wanted it to remain in ruins.

Now, [let us look at] the metaphorical interpretation that God does not elect all the gentiles, nor hate all the Jews, but chooses certain ones from among both. This testimony of Paul (Romans 9,24) serves less in refuting the freedom of the will, than in dampening the arrogance of the Jews, who believed that the Gospel's grace was to be theirs alone by virtue of their descent from Abraham. They abhorred the gentiles and did not wish to admit them to the community of evangelical grace. This Paul explains: "Even us whom he has called not only from among the Jews but also from among the gentiles" (Romans 9,24). Since God hates and loves only with righteous justification, hatred and love are no more standing in the way of free will, whether happening before or after the birth of man. When He already hates a man before his birth, it is because He knows for sure that he will do something odious; when after his birth, it is because he is actually doing something hateful. The Jews, who had been God's chosen people, have been rejected. The gentiles, on the other hand, not being the chosen people, have been received. Why have the Jews been cut off from the olive tree? Because they did not want to believe. And why have the gentiles been grafted unto it? Because they obeyed the Gospels. Paul himself gives us that reason: "They were broken off because of unbelief" (Romans 11,20), i.e., because they did not want to believe. Furthermore, [Paul] awakens hope in the broken-off branch that it could again be grafted on, if people would abandon their disbelief and would wish to believe. He warns the grafted-on branch that it might be chopped off, if it would turn away from the grace of God. "Whereas thou by faith standest. Be not high-minded, but fear" (Romans 11,20), and again, "Lest you should be wise in your own conceits" (Romans 11,25). It is quite evident that Paul's purpose is to dampen the conceit of gentiles as well as of Jews.

39) *Third Scriptural Passage: Clay in the Potter's Hand*

A third scriptural passage [of the opponents] is Isaiah 45, 9;

> *Woe to him that gainsayeth his maker, a shard of the earthen pots! Shall the clay say to him that fashioned it: what art thou making, and thy work is without hands?*

And even more explicitly in Jeremiah 18,6:

> *Can't I do with you as this potter, O house of Israel? Behold, as clay is in the hand of the potter, so are you in my hand.*

These passages are to prove more in Paul, than they intended to prove in the original writings of the prophets. Paul interprets them thus.[10]

> *Or is not the potter master of his clay, to make from the same mass one vessel for honorable, another for ignoble use? But what if God, wishing to show his wrath and to make known his power, endured with much patience vessels of wrath, ready for destruction, that he might show the riches of his glory upon vessels of mercy, which he has prepared unto glory?*

In both quotations the prophets rebuke the people murmuring against the Lord, while afflicted for their own betterment, just as Paul rejects their godless talk by exclaiming, "O man who art thou to reply to God?" (Romans 9,20). In this case we are obliged to submit to God, like moist clay to the potter's hands. Truly, our free will is thereby not completely cancelled out, because it is not impossible for our will to work together with the divine will for our eternal salvation. Thus follows in Jeremias soon the exhortation to do penance. We have already

---

[10]   Romans 9, 21-23.

quoted this passage.[11] It would be a useless exhortation if everything happened of necessity.

Paul aims not at completely excluding free will, but rather aims at rebuffing the godlessly grumbling Jews, who have been rejected from the grace of the Gospels on account of their obstinate unbelief, while the gentiles have been accepted because of their faith. It is obvious from the following passage in 2 Timothy 2,20-21:

> *But in a great house there are vessels not only of gold and silver, but also of wood and clay; and some are for honorable uses, but some for ignoble. If anyone, therefore, has cleansed himself from these, he will be a vessel for honorable use, sanctified and useful to the Lord, ready for every good work.*

Such parables used in Holy Scripture are very instructive, but are not applicable in all instances. How stupid to say to a chamberpot of Samian clay, "if you keep yourself clean, you will be a useful and noble vessel." It makes sense, however, to say this to a vessel endowed with intellect. After such an admonition it can accommodate itself to the will of the Lord. Because otherwise, if man would really be only for God what the clay is in the potter's hand, no one but the potter could be held responsible for the vessel, especially, if the potter himself has also mixed and conditioned the clay according to his will. Consequently, a vessel incapable of self-determination, and thus incapable of guilt, would be thrown into eternal fire.

Let us therefore interpret the parable as one employed for explaining grace. Because if we wish to apply all parts of it superstitiously to our opinion, we would be saying many ridiculous things. The potter makes vessels to be abused, but not before their preceding guilt. So he has discarded some Jews on account of their disbelief. Conversely, he has created among the gentiles vessels for noble use, on account of their faith. If one wants to drive us into a corner with scriptural quotations and wishes to take

---

[11]   Jeremiah 18, 8 ff. See also its quotation on p. 30.

the parable of the potter and his clay literally, why do they not permit us also this concluding sentence: "If any one, therefore, has cleansed himself" (2 Timothy 2,21). This would amount to a contradiction in Paul. While he makes in a preceding passage everything depend on the hand of God, here he places everything in the hands of man. Nevertheless, both passages are sound. One has this, the other that action in mind: the former wants to stop godless grumbling, the latter wishes to awaken zeal, and to protect as much from [a false sense of] security as from despair.

40) *Other Similar Passages*

Similarly it is in Isaiah 10,15:

> *Shall the axe boast itself against him that cutteth with it? Or shall the saw exalt itself against him by whom it was drawn? As if a rod should lift itself up against him that lifteth it up, and a staff exalt itself, which is but wood.*

These words are directed against a godless king whose hardness God uses to chastise his people. He ascribed to his own wisdom and strength that which could only happen because God permitted it, although he was only a tool of divine wrath. Yes, he was a tool, but a living and intelligent one. If an axe and saw would be such, too, then it would make sense to say of them that together with the craftsman they work on something by themselves. Servants are, as Aristotle teaches, living tools of their masters. Such would also be axes, saws, hatchets, ploughs, if they could move on their own, like those tripods which Vulcan manufactured in such a manner that they could intervene in battle by themselves.[12] The master commands and orders what is needed. The servant can accomplish nothing without his master. Nevertheless nobody would say that a servant who obeys the commands of his master is completely inactive. Moreover, the parable, as employed, aims not at contra-

---

[12]   Read about the work of Hephaestus (Greek for Vulcan) in the *Iliad,* Bk. XVIII, 375 and 418 ff.

dicting the freedom of the will, but at dampening the arrogance of a godless king who ascribes to his power and wisdom, rather than to God, what he had accomplished.

It is also not difficult to refute the proof which Origen cites from Ezekiel 36,26: "I will take away the stony heart out of your flesh, and will give you a heart of flesh." This is a metaphor. Similarly a teacher could say to a pupil with deficient Latin, "I'll drive that barbaric manner of speech out of you yet, and will drum classical Latin into you." Nonetheless [the teacher] would have to demand industriousness of his student, even while the latter could not learn to speak differently, except with the help of the teacher. What is a stony heart? It is a rude heart, stubbornly malicious. And what is a heart of flesh? It is a docile heart, obeying divine grace. Assuming a free will, it is nonetheless manifest that an obstinate heart cannot soften to true penance except with the aid of heavenly grace. He who grants docility demands that you exert yourself to be taught.

41) *Union of Grace and Freedom*

David prayed, "Create a pure heart in me" (Psalm 50,2). Paul in turn says: "If anyone has cleansed himself" (2 Timothy 2,21). Ezekiel exclaims: "Make yourself a new heart, and a new spirit" (Ezekiel 18,31). David in turn cries out: "And a resolute spirit renew within me" (Psalm 50,12) and prays: "And blot out all my iniquities" (Psalm 50,11). John in turn says: "And everyone who has this hope in him makes himself holy just as he also is holy" (1 John 3,3). David begs: "Deliver me from the penalty of blood" (Psalm 50,16). A prophet calls out: "Loose the bonds from thy neck, O captive daughter of Sion" (Isaias 52,2). Also Paul: "Let us therefore lay aside the works of darkness" (Romans 13,12). Also Peter: "Lay aside therefore all malice, and all deceit, and pretense . . ." (1 Peter 2,1). Paul says: "Work out your salvation with fear and trembling" (Philippians 2,12), though in 1 Corinthians 12,6 he says: "[He is] the same God, who works all things in all."

More than six hundred such proofs can be found in Holy Scripture. If man could effect nothing, why do they admonish us to work? If man can effect something, why say that God alone works all things in all? By utilizing and distorting one set of passages, man appears impotent. By emphasizing in partiality the other set, man will be doing everything. Now, if man could do nothing, there would be no room for merit and guilt; consequently also none for punishment and reward. If on the other hand man were to do all, there would be no room for grace, which is very often mentioned and emphasized by Paul. The Holy Spirit can not contradict himself. The canonical books of Holy Scripture originated under his inspiration. Their inviolable sublimity is acknowledged and affirmed by both parties in the dispute. Therefore one must find an interpretation which resolves this seeming contradiction.

Whoever wants to abolish the freedom of the will, will be interpreting "Stretch forth thy hand to which thou wilt" (Ecclesiasticus 15,17) to signify that grace will stretch out its hand according to its will. "Make yourself a new heart" (Ezekiel 18,31) signifies that the grace of God will create for you a new heart. "And everyone who has this hope in him makes himself holy" (1 John 3,3) signifies that grace sanctifies him. "Let us therefore lay aside the works of darkness" (Romans 15,12) signifies that grace may lay them aside. Very often we read in Holy Scripture he has done justice, he has done inequity. One would have to interpret this to mean that God has exercised justice in one and has done injustice in the other.

If I were now to propose the interpretation of orthodox Church Fathers or Church Councils, I would soon be interrupted with the objection that these are only human.[13] And I am not permitted to say against the most violent and distorted interpretation of Luther that he too is only

---

[13] Recall the argument of Erasmus, the Humanist, concerning "human" in chapter I.

human? Of course, the opponent would be victorious, were it permissible to interpret Scripture according to his momentary whim, while we would not be permitted to follow the interpretations of the Church Fathers, nor produce our own.

The passage "stretch forth thy hand to which thou wilt" (Ecclesiasticus 15,17) is, of course, so clear that it needs no interpretation. It means that grace will stretch out your hand at will.[14] The interpretation of the most trustworthy Doctors of the Church, on the contrary, must be a dream, if we do not want to call it the imputation of Satan, as others did.

Now, the quoted passages which seem to contradict each other are easily reconciled, if we join together our will with the help of divine grace. Instead of this clear solution when mentioning the parable of the potter (Isaias 45,9), and the axe (Isaias 10,15), they attack us with words which they want to be understood literally, since this is advantageous to their cause. Yet in this other case, they abandon unhesitatingly the words of Holy Scripture, and offer an interpretation which is almost as bold as saying, "[Pope] Peter wrote," while another interprets this as meaning that someone else in the house writes and not he, Peter.

---

[14]   Is meant ironically, of course. This frequent type of jocundity belongs to the Humanist style just as do the Humanists' antipathies for scholastic subtleties and dialectical complexities, and their love for pagan classics, stylistic predilection, and witty disputation.

VI

LUTHER'S PROOFS AGAINST THE FREE WILL

WE WANT to examine[1] now how valid are Martin Luther's [arguments] with which he wishes to topple the freedom of the will from its throne.

42) *Weakness of Human Nature*

He quotes a passage from Genesis: "My spirit shall not remain in man forever, since he is flesh" (Genesis 6,3). Scripture understands by "flesh" here not simply a godless passion, as Paul sometimes uses it when commanding the mortification of the flesh,[2] but rather the weakness of our nature inclined towards sin, as Paul again implies when he calls the Corinthians carnal, as little children in Christ, with no capacity yet for solid doctrines.[3]

Moreover Jerome remarks in his *Hebraic Questions*[4] that the Hebrew differs from our Latin text, namely, "my spirit will not judge these men in eternity, because they are [merely] flesh." These words betray God's gentleness rather than severity. "Flesh" refers to man, by nature weak and inclined to evil. In turn God's wrath is called "spirit."

---

[1] Here the reader will find a strong reliance on the Bishop of Rochester, Fisher's treatment. Cf. chapter I, footnote 4.

[2] Romans 8, 13.

[3] 1 Corinthians 3, 1 ff.

[4] Cf. chapter II, footnote 1. The so-called Hebraic questions of investigations are found in Jerome's *De situ et nominibus hebraicorum,* which is a translation of the *Onomasticon* of Eusebius, with Jerome's additions and corrections.

Accordingly, God affirms he does not want to retain man
for eternal punishment, but rather out of mercy [he wants]
to punish him already here [on earth]. This utterance
refers not to all mankind, but only to the men of those days,
terribly corrupted by abominable vices. It states explicitly
"these men." God did not just refer to all men of those
days, because Noah, for example, was praised as a just man
agreeable to God.

43) *Inclination to Evil*

One can contradict in the same way [what Luther
quotes]: "The inclination of man's heart is evil from his
youth" (Genesis 8,21), and "Man's every thought and all
the inclination of his heart were only evil" (Genesis 6,5).
The tendency towards evil existing in most men does not
completely cancel out the freedom of the will, even when
one cannot overcome evil without the help of divine grace.
If, however, a change of mind depends never on the human
will, but everything is accomplished by God according to
some necessity, why has man then been granted a time
interval for doing penance? "His lifetime shall be one
hundred and twenty years" (Genesis 6,3). According to
Jerome's *Hebraic Questions* this passage refers not to the
lifetime of man, but to the time of the Great Flood. It was
offered to man, as a chance of changing their minds, if they
wished to. Or if they did not wish to, to merit divine
punishment as a people contemptuous of the Lord's
leniency.

44) *Forgiving Grace*

Furthermore [Luther] quotes Isaias 40,2: "She hath
received of the Lord double for all her sins." Jerome interprets this as referring to divine punishment and not the
forgiveness of sin. True, Paul says: "Where the offenses
have abounded, grace has abounded yet more" (Romans
5,20). It does not follow from this that before the reception

of sanctifying grace man cannot prepare himself with the help of God and morally good works for the favor of divine grace. We read of the centurion Cornelius, who was not yet baptized nor filled with the Holy Spirit: "Thy prayers and thy alms have gone up and have been remembered in the sight of God" (Acts 10,4). If all works done before the reception of the highest grace were evil, is it then evil works that must gain God's favor for us?

45) *Spirit and Flesh*

From the same chapter in Isaias [Luther] also quotes (Isaias 40,6-8):

> *All flesh is grace, and all glory thereof as the flower of the field. The grass is withered, and the flower is fallen, because the spirit of the Lord has blown upon it . . . But the Lord endureth forever.*

It seems to me that this passage has been forced [by Luther] to refer to grace and free will. Jerome maintains that "spirit" signifies divine wrath, and "flesh" the natural weakness of man, which has no power against God, and "flower" the vainglory resulting from good luck in material transactions. The Jews prided themselves in their temple, their circumcision, their sacrifice,[5] and the Greeks prided themselves in their wisdom.[6] Since, however, the wrath of God has manifested itself in the Gospel, all this pride and haughtiness has come to naught.

But man is not entirely flesh. There are, too, the soul and the spirit by which we strive towards the honorable. This part of the soul we call reason, or ἡγεμονικόν, i.e., the directive faculty. Or should one presume that philosophers did not strive for the honorable, though they taught it to be a thousand times better to suffer death than commit an infamous action, even if we could know beforehand that men would not notice and God would forgive it? But fallen

---

[5]   Romans 2, 17 ff.

[6]   1 Corinthians 1, 22.

nature judges often wrongly, as the Lord says, "You do not know of what manner of spirit you are" (Luke 9, 55).[7]

It was just such an erroneous judgment when the disciples, desiring revenge, appealed to the story of Elias requesting heavenly fire to consume two leaders with their fifty men.[8] Even in good men the human spirit is different from God's Spirit, as Paul says: "The Spirit himself gives testimony to our spirit that we are sons of God" (Romans 8,16). If someone wants to contend that even the most distinguished human quality is nothing but flesh, i.e. a godless disposition, it would be easy to agree, except that he first prove this assertion from Scripture.

"That which is born of the flesh is flesh, and that which is born of the Spirit is spirit" (John 3,6). John teaches that those who believe the Gospels are born of God (1 John 5,1) and become children of God (John 1,12), yes, even gods (John 10,34). And Paul distinguishes the carnal man who does not understand the divine, from the spiritual who judges everything rightly.[9] And on another occasion he speaks again of a new creature in Christ.[10] If the entire man, even the one reborn through faith, were nothing else but flesh,[11] where is the spirit born of Spirit, the fact of being children of God, and the new creature? I wish to be enlightened on that! Until then I like to appeal to the authority of the Church Fathers who teach that certain germinal concepts of the ethical good are within man by

---

[7]   This passage seems a good example of the Erasmian spirit of common sense and conciliation. He wants to avoid the extremes on either side of the controversy. He seems to be saying: man is not all flesh; with his reason he can strive for many good things; but reason is dimmed by the fallen nature of man; therefore man's reason needs the enlightenment of God's Spirit. This is the burden of the quotes from Luke and Paul.

[8]   Luke 9, 54.

[9]   1 Corinthians 2, 14 ff.

[10]   2 Corinthians 5, 17.

[11]   This is not precisely what Luther would say, but a typical example of Renaissance liking for exaggeration. Though Erasmus decries this, he, too, falls prey to it at times.

his nature, and that he consequently recognizes and follows in some way the ethical good, although coarser inclinations are added, enticing him to the opposite.

Finally, the will capable of turning here and there is generally called a free will, despite its more ready assent to evil than to good, because of our remaining inclination to sin. Yet no one is forced to do evil unless he consents.

46) *Divine Guidance*

Luther then quotes from Jeremiah: "I know, O Lord, that the way of a man is not his; neither is it in a man to walk, and to direct his steps" (Jeremiah 10,23). This pertains to the occurrence of happy and unhappy circumstances, rather than the possibility of a free will. Frequently man plunges profoundly into misfortune, when he is very careful to avoid it. This does not eliminate the freedom of the will—neither among those hit by misfortune, because they did not forsee its coming, nor among those causing it, because they don't humiliate the enemy with the same intention as does God, namely by castigating. If one nonetheless forces these words to apply to the freedom of the will, everyone would have to admit that without the grace of God nobody can keep the right course in life. Our daily prayer is: "Lord, my God, make smooth thy way before me" (Psalm 5,9). Nonetheless, we continue to strive with all our strength. We pray: "Incline, O God, my heart to thy precepts" (Psalm 118,36). Whoever begs for help does not abandon his undertaking.

Furthermore [Luther] quotes: "It is the part of man to prepare the soul and of the Lord to govern the tongue" (Proverbs 16,1). [I say:] This also concerns what can happen or does not happen, without him thereby loosing eternal salvation. But how could man resolve this [freely] in his heart, when Luther firmly maintains that everything happens of necessity? In the same chapter it says: "Lay open thy works to the Lord, and thy thoughts shall be directed" (Proverbs 16,3). It reads "thy works" and "thy thoughts." Both words could not be said, if God works everything in us, both good and evil. "By mercy and truth iniquity is redeemed" (Proverbs 16,6). These and many other passages from the Proverbs support the acceptance of a free will.

Now, [Luther] quotes from the same chapter: "The Lord hath made all things for himself; the wicked also for the evil day" (Proverbs 16,4). [I answer:] God has created nothing evil by its nature. Nevertheless in his unfathomable wisdom he turns all things, even evil, to our advantage and to his glory. Even Lucifer was not created as the evil one, but rather, since his voluntary defection, God set him aside for eternal punishment, in order to train the pious ones by his malice, and to punish the godless.

It does not become any more difficult when [Luther] quotes: "As the divisions of waters, so the heart of the king is in the hand of the Lord" (Proverbs 21,1). [I say:] The one who guides does not necessarily force. Nonetheless, as mentioned before, nobody denies that God could forcefully influence the thinking capacity of man, expel his original intentions and inculcate another, yes, even deprive him of his intellect. But this does not change the fact that normally speaking our wills are free.

If that is Solomon's opinion which Luther here interprets, namely that all hearts are in the hand of the Lord, why does he proclaim it to be something special with the heart of a king? This passage agrees even more so with what we read in Job 34,30: "Who maketh a man that is a hypocrite to reign for the sins of the people?" The same in Isaias 3,4: "And I will give children to be their princes, and the effeminate shall rule over them." When God, propitious to his people, inclines the heart of a king towards good, he is not necessarily forcing the will. Instead, to incline [the heart] to evil means that [God] offended by the sins of a people, does not recall the soul of a foolish, rapacious, warring and despotic prince [to come to his senses], but permits him to be senselessly driven by his passions, in order to castigate the people through [the king's] malice. Should it happen that God drives such a guilty king to evil, it would be wrong to form a generalization from such a special case.

Such proofs as Luther assembles then from the Proverbs could be gathered in huge numbers. But this would serve more their accumulation than their victory. Rhetoricians generally throw such arguments about them. Most of the time these can be applied conveniently to an interpretation favorable to free will, or to one against it.

47) *Nothing without Christ*

Luther considers Christ's saying in John 15,5: "Without me you can do nothing," just as accurate a javelin as the one Achilles used. In my opinion it is possible to respond in more than one way. First, "unable to do" usually means to be unable to reach what one strives for. This does not exclude the possibility of the striver proceeding in some way just the same. In this sense it is completely correct that we can do nothing without Christ. He speaks of the evangelical fruit which can be found only among those who abide in the life on the vine, i.e. in Jesus Christ. Paul uses this mode of speaking when he says: "So then neither he who plants is anything, nor he who waters, but God who gives the growth" (1 Corinthians 3,7). That which is considered of little moment and is of no value is called "nothing." The same: "[If I] do not have charity, I am nothing" (1 Corinthians 13,2). Followed by: ". . . it profits me nothing" (1 Corinthians 13,3), and again: "He calls things that are not as though they were" (Romans 4,17). Once more, he calls, according to Osee, those who are not his people, despised and rejected ones.[12] A similar mode of expression is contained in the Psalms: "I am a worm and not a man" (Psalm 21,7).

If one were to press this expression "nothing," then it would not be possible to sin without Christ. I believe Christ means here his grace, if one does not want to escape to an

---

[12] Romans 9, 25 ff quoting Osee 1, 9 and 2, 24.

already discarded [view] that sin is nothing [real]. Yet even this [not being without Christ] is in a sense correct, since without Christ we would neither be here, nor live, nor move. [My opponents] grant that sometimes the free will without grace is capable of sin. Even Luther has held this at the beginning of his *Assertio*.

VII

POSTSCRIPT ON APPARENT PROOFS AGAINST THE FREE WILL

48) *Reasonable Interpretation of Additional Passages*[1]

Here belong the words of John the Baptist "No one can receive anything unless it is given to him from heaven" (John 3,27). Hence it does not follow that we lack the faculty or use of free will. The fact that fire warms us, comes from heaven; the fact that we seek by a natural impulse the useful and avoid the harmful, comes from heaven; the fact that after sin the will is excited to better efforts comes from heaven; the fact that we can obtain grace pleasing to God through our tears, almsgiving and prayers, comes from heaven. In the meantime our will is not inactive, even if man can reach the goal of his striving only with the final assistance of grace. But since it is a minimum which we contribute, the entire affair is attributed to God. Just as a mariner steering his ship safely through a heavy storm into port does not say, "I have saved my ship," but rather "God has saved it." Nevertheless his art and zeal were not idle. Similarly, a farmer does not say when taking a rich harvest into his barn, "I have produced this year's rich harvest," but rather "God has given it." Who would say, however, that the farmer has contributed

---

[1] This refers to the passage on grace (John 3, 27), God speaking through men (Matthew 10, 20), the pulling power of grace (John 6, 44), thinking in God, but living in man (2 Corinthians 3, 5), and the origin of all good to be found in God (1 Corinthians 4, 7).

nothing to the prospering of the fruits of the earth? Among common sayings are these: God has given you beautiful children, though their father has helped to generate them; God restored my health, though the doctor helped along; the king has overcome his enemies, though generals and soldiers have contributed their good share. Nothing can grow, if heaven does not send the rain. Nevertheless, good soil produces good fruits, while bad soil can produce no good fruits. But since human endeavor alone accomplishes nothing without divine help, everything is attributed to divine benefaction. "Unless the Lord build the house, they labor in vain who build it. Unless the Lord guard the city, the guards watch in vain" (Psalms 126,1). In the meantime the builders and the guards do not cease in their building and in their vigilance.

Furthermore in Matthew 10,20: "For it is not you who are speaking, but the Spirit of your Father who speaks through you." This passage seems at first sight to annul the freedom of the will. But in fact it wants to free us from distressing anxiety, when premeditating on what to say in behalf of Christ. Otherwise it would be a sin, if preachers were to prepare themselves carefully for their sacred sermons. Not everyone should expect that, because the Spirit once inspired uncouth disciples, he too would be able to preach as if he had been given the gift of tongues. This may have happened once, nonetheless [the recipient] had to conform his will to the inspiration of the Holy Spirit, and acted together with him. This is obviously the duty of the free will. Or should we assume that God has spoken to us through the mouth of the Apostles, as he did with Balaam through the mouth of a donkey?[2]

A passage from John could drive us further into the corner: "No one can come to me unless the Father who sent me draw him" (John 6,44). The word "draw" seems to point to necessity and exclude the free will. But actually it is a nonviolent drawing. It causes a person to want a

---

[2] Numbers 22, 23 ff.

thing just as readily as he can refuse it. And as we show a little boy an apple and he comes running; a sheep a willow twig and it follows, so God moves our soul by his grace and we give ourselves willingly.

In the same way is to be understood what John says: "No one comes to the Father but through me" (John 14,6). As the father glorifies the son, and the son the father, so the father draws [us humans] to the son, and the son to the father. Yet we are drawn in such a way that we soon run willingly. Thus we read: "Draw me: we will run after thee" (Canticles 1,3).

In the Pauline letters there are also passages which seem to destroy completely any influence of the free will. "Not that we are sufficient of ourselves to think anything, as from ourselves, but our sufficiency is from God" (2 Corinthians 3,5). One can save the free will in two ways here.

First, several orthodox [Church] Fathers distinguished three steps in human action: (1) thinking, (2) willing and (3) doing. In the first and third steps they attributed no operation to the free will. Grace alone causes our Spirit to think good things; by grace alone is he guided to carry out the thought. But in the middle step, i.e., the willingness, both grace and human will are effective. The main cause is grace, and the secondary one our will. Since the whole is attributed to the one who has executed all things, it is improper of man to claim a good action for himself, since even the fact that he consented and cooperated with divine grace, is God's gift.

Secondly, the preposition "from" points to the origin and source, and therefore Paul distinctly states "of ourselves" as "from ourselves," i.e., "out of ourselves."[3] This could also be said by someone who admits man to be able to effect good by natural powers, since he does not possess these of himself either.

For who would deny that all good has its origin in God

---

[3] Erasmus distinguishes in his text *a nobis* from *ex nobis*, Paul using the former, by explaining with the Greek ἀφ᾽ ἑαυτῶν ὡς ἐξ ἑαυτῶν.

as a source? Paul inculcates this, in order to deprive us of
our arrogance and overconfidence, as also when he says:
"What hast thou that thou hast not received? And if thou
hast received it, why dost thou boast as if thou hast not
received it?" (1 Corinthians 4,7). You hear vainglory being
restrained in this saying. This is what the servant, too,
would hear who accounted to his master for the profit made
on usury.[4] If he attributed to himself his well-invested
labors, [the master may ask] what have you received that
you did not possess? And nevertheless, the master praises
him for his untiring strenuous efforts.

The same song is sung in James 1,17: "Every good gift
and every perfect gift is from above," and Paul in Ephesians
1,11: "Him who works all things according to the counsel
of his will." These words aim at this that we should not
arrogate anything to us, but attribute everything to the
grace of God who has called us while we turned away from
him, has cleansed us through faith, and who has also
granted that our will can cooperate with his grace, although
the latter by itself would be completely sufficient and in
no need of any help coming from the human will.

49) *To Rule and to Effect*

The passage in Philippians 2,13, "For it is God who of
his own good pleasure works in you both the will and the
performance," does not exclude the free will. If you relate
"of his good pleasure" to man, as Ambrose of Milan does,
you'll understand that the good will cooperates with the
effective grace. Just before (Philippians 2,12) we read:
"Work out your salvation with fear and trembling." One
can conclude from this that both God works in us, and that
our will and effort strive solicitously with God. Nobody
should have to reject this interpretation, because, as stated,
immediately preceding is the passage "work out your salvation"—ἐργάζεσθε, which signifies more correctly "to toil,"
than the word ἐνεργεῖν, which is attributed to God, God

---

[4]   Matthew 25, 20 ff.

being ὁ ἐνεργῶν, the one who effects and rules. But ἐνεργεῖ refers to that which effects and impels. But even granted that both ruling and effecting mean the same, this passage teaches us clearly that both God and man work.

What could man effect if our will were the same for God as the clay for the potter? "For it is not you who are speaking, but the spirit of your father who speaks through you" (Matthew 10,20).[5] This was said to the Apostles. Nevertheless we read in the Acts: "Then Peter, filled with the Holy Spirit, said to them" (Acts 4,8). How could the two contradictory statements be reconciled, according to which not man, but the Spirit speaks, and accordingly to which Peter speaks filled with the Holy Spirit, unless the Spirit speaks in the Apostles in such a manner that at one and the same time while speaking obediently to the Spirit it is also true that they do not speak, not in the sense of not acting [i.e., making speech], but in the sense that they are not the first cause of their sermons.

We also read about Stephen: "And they were not able to withstand the wisdom and the spirit who spoke" (Acts 6,10). And yet he himself spoke before the Sanhedrin. Paul says: "It is now no longer I that live, but Christ lives in me" (Galatians 2,20), and nevertheless, according to Paul the just man lives by faith (Romans 1,17). How is it that he does not live, when he is living? Because he ascribes it to the Spirit of God that he is living.

Equally: "Yet not I, but the grace of God within me" (1 Corinthians 15,10). If Paul had done nothing, why did he state before that he has done something? Not only that, he even said: "In fact I have labored more than many of them" (1 Corinthians 15,10). If it is true what he says, why does he correct this, as if he had spoken incorrectly? The correction obviously does not intend that one should think he had done nothing, but he wanted to avoid the appearance of having attributed to his own strength what he had accomplished with the help of divine grace. The

---

[5] Cf. Erasmus, Section 48.

correction aimed at the suspicion of insolence and not at the possibility of cooperation in action.

God does not want man to attribute everything to himself, not even when he merits it. "When you have done everything that was commanded you, say "we are unprofitable servants: we have done what it was our duty to do¹" (Luke 17,10). Would he not distinguish himself who keeps all the commandments of God? I do not know whether such a man can be found anywhere. And yet, those who might accomplish this are told to say "we are unworthy servants." Nobody denies their accomplishments; rather are they taught to avoid dangerous arrogance.

Man says one thing, God another. Man says he is a servant, an unworthy one at that. What does God say? "Well done, good servant" (Luke 19,17); "No longer do I call you servants, but friends" (John 15,15). He calls them "brethren" (John 20,17) instead of "servants." And those who call themselves unworthy servants, God calls his sons.⁶ And indeed those who have just called themselves servants God summons: "Come, blessed of my Father" (Matthew 25,34), and they hear of their good deed, of which they themselves knew nothing.

I believe it to be an excellent key to the understanding of Holy Scriptures, if we pay attention to what is meant in each passage. Once one recognizes this, one will find it proper to select from the parables and examples such as are to the point. In the parable of the steward, who about to be relieved of his post, falsifies the notes of his master's debtors, there is much that does not add to the sense of the parable.⁷ Only this can be gathered from it, that everyone should strive to distribute most freely, thereby aiding his neighbor, the gifts he has received from God, before death overtake him.

The same concerns the parable we just mentioned above:

---

⁶ Romans 9, 26.
⁷ Luke 16, 1-9.

> *But which of you is there, having a servant plowing or tending sheep, who will say to him on his return from the field, "Come at once and recline at table!" But will he not say to him, "Prepare my supper, and gird thyself and serve me till I have eaten and drunk; and afterwards thou thyself shalt eat and drink?" Does he thank that servant for doing what he commanded him? I do not think so.*

The sum total of this parable is that one ought simply to obey the commandments of God and do zealously one's duty without claiming any praise for it.

Otherwise the Lord himself dissents from this parable when he gives himself as a servant, while granting his disciples the honor of reclining at table.[8] He also expresses thanks when he exclaims: "Well done good servants" (Luke 19,17), and "Come blessed" (Matthew 25,34). Thus, he is not saying: "The Lord will judge you unworthy of grace, unprofitable servants, after you have done everything," but rather says: "You say, we are unprofitable servants" (Luke 17,10). Paul who worked more than all the rest calls himself the least among the Apostles and unworthy to be called Apostle.[9]

Similarly: "Are not two sparrows sold for a farthing? And yet not one of them will fall to the ground without your Father's leave" (Matthew 10,29). First we must bear in mind what the Lord is discussing. He does not wish to teach the so-called forced necessity of all happenings. His example aims rather at taking from his disciples their fear of men. They should realize that they stand under God's protection, and that no man can harm them without his permission. This he will only do if it furthers them and the gospel. Paul says: "Is it for the oxen that God has care?" (1 Corinthians 9,9). Obviously the subsequent remarks of the Evangelist contain an hyperbole, i.e. an oratorical exaggeration, "As for you, the very hairs of your head are all numbered" (Matthew 10,30). How much

---

[8] John 13, 4 ff.
[9] 1 Corinthians 15, 9.

hair falls daily to the ground; is it also counted? So, what is the purpose of this hyperbole? Obviously that which follows it, "Therefore, do not be afraid" (Matthew 10,21). Just as these modes of expression have the purpose to remove the fear of man and to strengthen his trust in God, without whose providence nothing happens, so the above quotations do not purport to abolish the free will, but to deter us from arrogance which the Lord hates. The best is to attribute everything to the Lord. He is mild and will not only give what is ours, but also that which belongs to him.

How could one state that the prodigal son[10] had squandered his portion of the property, if he never had a part of it in his hands? What he possessed he had received from the father. We too acknowledge that all the gifts of nature are gifts of God. He possessed his portion even at the time his father has still retained it in his hands and indeed possessed it more securely. What does it mean that he demanded his portion and separated himself from his father? Obviously it means that man claims title for himself to the gifts of nature, and does not use them to fulfill God's commandments, but to satisfy his carnal desires. What is the meaning of this hunger? It means an affliction by which God goads on the sinner's disposition to know and to abhor himself, and to undertake the desired return to the father. What signifies the son speaking to himself, planning to confess and to return home? It signifies the will of man turning towards grace, which has stimulated him, and which, as stated, one calls the prevenient one.[11] What signifies the father who hastens to meet his son? He signifies the grace of God which furthers our will, so that we can accomplish that which we wish.

This interpretation, even if it were my own invention, would certainly be more probable than that of my opponents who interpret "stretch forth thy hand to which thou

---

[10]   Cf. Luke 15, 11 f.
[11]   Cf. chapter III, footnote 3 and 11.

wilt" (Ecclesiasticus 15,17) to mean, "the grace of God stretches out your hand at will," only in order to "prove" that the will of man can accomplish nothing.[12] Since my interpretation, however, is handed down from the orthodox Fathers, I do not see why one should despise it. This pertains also to the poor widow placing her two mites, i.e., her entire property, into the treasury.[13]

I ask, what merit can he gain who owes completely to him from whom he received these forces all he is able to do by his natural intelligence and free will? Nevertheless, God credits us precisely with this that we do not turn our hearts away from his grace, and that we concentrate our natural abilities on simple obedience. This proves at least that man can accomplish something, but that nevertheless he ascribes the sum total of all his doings to God, who is the author whence orginates man's ability to unite his striving to God's grace. This is what Paul means, when he says: "By the grace of God I am what I am" (1 Corinthians 15,10). He recognizes the author. But when you hear, "His grace has not been fruitless" (ibid.), then you recognize the human will, whose striving cooperates with divine help. The same is indicated when it says: "Not I, but the grace of God with me" (ibid.). For in Greek it is ἡ σὺν ἐμοί.

And the Hebrew prophet of wisdom wished that divine wisdom assist him; standing at his side and working with him.[14] She assists as a moderator and helper, like an architect supporting his assistant, ordering what is to be done, showing the correct method. If he commences to do something wrongly, she will recall him, and as soon as he fails, she hastens to his aid. The work is ascribed to the architect, without whose help nothing could have been accomplished. Nevertheless nobody would say, that helpers and apprentices have no share in the work whatsoever. What the architect is for the apprentice, grace is for our will.

---

[12]   Cf. Erasmus, Section 41.
[13]   Mark 12, 41 ff.
[14]   Wisdom 9, 10.

Therefore Paul says. "In like manner the Spirit also helps our weakness" (Romans 8,26). One does not call another weak who can do nothing, but one whose strength is insufficient for completing his undertaking. Nor is he called a helper who does everything alone. All Scripture exclaims: help, aid, assistance and support. But who could be designated as helper unless he helped one doing something? The potter does not "help" the clay in the forming of a vessel, nor the carpenter his axe in the making of a bench.

50) *Free Will and Good Works Made Possible through Grace*

We oppose those who conclude like this: "Man is unable to accomplish anything unless God's grace helps him. Therefore there are no good works of man." We propose the rather more acceptable conclusion: Man is able to accomplish all things, if God's grace aids him. Therefore it is possible that all works of man be good.

As many passages as there are in Holy Scripture mentioning [God's] help, as many are there establishing the freedom of the will. These passages are innumerable. I would have won already, if it depended on the mere number of proofs.

VIII

SUMMARY AND CONCLUSION

51) *Need for a Moderate Opinion*

Up to now we have been compiling scriptural passages establishing the freedom of the will, while conversely others seem to cancel it out completely. Since the Holy Spirit, who inspired both, can not contradict himself, we are forced, whether we like it or not, to seek a more moderate opinion.

When one has arrived at this view, others at that view, both reading the same Scripture, it is due to the fact that each looked for something else and interpreted that which he read for his own purpose. Whoever pondered the great religious indifference of man and the great danger of despairing of salvation, has, while trying to avert this calamity, succumbed unsuspectingly to another danger, and has ascribed too much to the free will. The others instead—who considered how enormously dangerous for true piety the trust of man in his own prowess and merits can be, and how unbearable the arrogance of certain persons is who boast of their good works and sell them to others according to measurement and weight like selling oil and soap—having very studiously avoided this danger, have either diminished the freedom of the will so that it could contribute absolutely nothing to good works, or they have eliminated it all together by introducing an absolute necessity in all happenings.

52) *Some Reformers' Views Justified*

Evidently these people considered it quite apt for the simple obedience of a Christian that man depend completely on the will of God when he places his entire trust and all his hopes in his promises; when he, conscious of his own wretchedness, admires and loves his immense mercy which he gives us plentifully without charge; when he, furthermore, subjects himself completely to his will, no matter whether he wants to save or destroy him; when he accepts no praise whatsover for his good works, and rather ascribes all glory to His grace, thinking that man is nothing else but a living tool of the divine Spirit, which the latter has cleansed and sanctified for himself through his undeserved goodness, and which he guides and governs according to his inscrutable wisdom; furthermore, when there exists nothing anybody could claim as his own accomplishment, and when he hopes for eternal life as reward for steadfast faith in God, not because he had earned it by his own good works, but because the goodness of God was pleased to promise that reward to those who have trust in him; whereby, consequently, man has the duty to beg God assiduously for imparting and augmenting his Spirit in us, to thank him for every success and to adore in all cases God's omnipotence, to admire everywhere his wisdom, and to love everywhere his goodness.

These utterances are also very praiseworthy to me, because they agree with Holy Scripture. They conform to the creed of those who died once and for all to this world, through their baptism have been buried with Christ, and after the mortification of the flesh live henceforth with the Spirit of Jesus, into whose body they have been ingrafted, through faith.[1] This is incontestably a pious and captivating conception, which takes from us every conceit, which transfers all glory and confidence to Christ, which expels from us the fear of men and demons, and which, though making

---

[1]   Meant is the Mystical Body of Christ, Cf. Romans 6, 4.

us distrustful of our human potentialities, makes us nonetheless strong and courageous in God. This we applaud
freely, up to the point of exaggeration [which we want to
avoid].

53) *Errors and Injustice in the Reformers*

But the rational soul in me has many doubts when I
hear the following: there is no merit in man; all his
works, even the pious ones, are sin; our will can do no
more than the clay in the potters hand; everything we do
or want to do is reduced to unconditional necessity.

First, why do you read so often that the saints, rich in
good work, have acted with justice, have walked upright
in the sight of God, never deviating to the right or to the
left, if everything is sin, even what the most pious does
—[in fact] such a sin that one for whom Christ has died
would nonetheless be condemned to inferno, were it not
for God's mercy?

Secondly, why does one so often hear of reward, if there
is no merit it all? How would disobedience of those following God's commandments be praised, and disobedience be
damned? Why does Holy Scripture so frequently mention
judgment, if merit cannot be weighed at all? Or why must
we stand before the seat of judgment if nothing has happened according to our will, but everything according to
mere necessity? It is disturbing to think of all the many
admonitions, commandments, threats, exhortations and
complaints, if we can do nothing, but God's unchangeable
will causes the willing as well as the carrying out in us.
He wants us to pray perseveringly. He wants us to watch,
to fight and to struggle for the reward of eternal life. Why
does he continuously want to be asked, when he has already decided whether to give us or not to give us, and
when he himself, unchangeable, is unable to change his
resolutions? Why does he command us to strive laboriously
for what he has decided to give freely? God's grace fights
and triumphs in us when we are afflicted, ejected, derided,

tortured and killed. Such atrocities the martyrs suffered. Nonetheless [such a martyr] is to have no merit. Indeed, it is called a sin, if he submits his body to tortures, in the hope of heavenly life. But why would an exceedingly merciful God wish to be thus engaged with his martyrs? Cruel would appear a man if he did not give, unless having tortured to despair, that which he had [already] decided to bestow freely upon his friend.

Perhaps, as soon as one confronts this obscurity in the divine decision, one ought to adore that which we are not supposed to comprehend, so that man says, "he is the Lord, he can do everything he wishes, and since he is by nature good, everything he wills can only be very good." It is still plausible enough to say that God crowns his gifts in us; he permits his benefits to be our advantage; he deigns with undeserved goodness to attribute to us what he has caused in us, well deserved, as it were, if we trust in him, and in order to obtain immortality. But I don't know how those can be consistent who exaggerate God's mercy towards the pious in such a way as to permit him to be almost cruel against the others.

A goodness which imputes to us its excellence might possibly be tolerable to a pious soul. But it is difficult to explain how it is compatible with justice (not to speak with mercy), to condemn the others, in whom God did not deign to cause good, to eternal tortures, although on their own they could not possibly effect any good, since they either possessed no free will, or only one good for sinning.

54) *Two Illustrative Stories*

If a king were to give enormous booty to one who had done nothing in a war, and to those who had done the fighting barely just their salary, he could respond to the murmuring soldiers: am I injuring you by giving the others freely and gratuitously? But really, how could one consider him just and gentle, if he crowned magnificently for his victory a general whom he had furnished with machines, troops, money and all supplies aplenty for war, while another, whom he had thrown into war without armaments, he ordered put to death on account of the war's unhappy ending? Before dying, could he not say with justice to the king: why do you punish me for what happened through your fault? If you had equipped me similarly, I would have won too.

Again, if a lord emancipates an undeserving servant, he can answer the remaining grumbling servants: You lose nothing if I am kind to this one; you still have your measure. Everybody would judge the lord cruel and unjust though, were he to have his servant flogged for his stature, or protruding nose, or some other lack of elegance. Would he not be justified in complaining against the lord who had him flogged: why should I suffer punishment for something that is not in my power to change? And he would be quite justified in saying this if it were in the lord's power to change the defects of the servant's body, just as it is in the hand of God to change our will. Or if the lord had given the servant that which now offends him, like cutting off his nose, or hideously deforming his face with scars, just as God, according to the opinion of some, has worked all evil in us. Or take the example of a lord giving orders to do a great deal to a servant lying in chains, "go here, do that, run, come back," and threatens him greatly if he were not to obey. But [the lord] did not set [the servant] loose, rather he flogged the disobedient fellow. Would not the servant justly consider the lord insane and cruel, if he had him flogged to death because he had not done that which was not in his power?

55) *Reservations Concerning Justification by Faith*

[Let us continue:] In this affair they greatly exalt faith and love of God. We hold these equally dear. We are convinced that the life of Christians is so contaminated with wickedness, stemming from nothing else but from the coldness and drowsiness of our faith which is a superficial belief in words, while, according to Paul, he is justified who within his heart believes. I do not especially want to quarrel with those who attribute everything to faith as the fountainhead, although it seems to me that faith and love, and love and faith come about and nurture each other mutually. Certainly faith is nurtured by love, as the flame in a lamp is nurtured by the oil. For we have greater faith in him whom we love dearly. There is no scarcity of voices who, more correctly, take faith as the beginning of salvation and not its sum total. But we don't want to argue about that.

56) *Exaggerating and Underrating*

But care should be taken not to deny the freedom of the will, while praising faith. For if this happens, there is no telling how the problem of divine justice and mercy could be solved.

The ancients could not explain such difficulties. Some felt compelled to assume two gods: one for the Old Testament, who was able to be only just, but not simultaneously merciful, and one for the New Testament, who could only be merciful, but not just. This godless idea Tertullian has sufficiently refuted.[2] Mani, as already mentioned,[3] fancied two natures in man, one which is incapable of not sinning, and one incapable of not doing good. Pelagius, who was concerned about God's justice, attributed more to free will than to necessity. Not too distant from this position are the [Scotists] who ascribe to human will at least the ability to earn with natural powers through ethically good works that highest grace, by which we are justified. They seem to me to be inviting man to strive by affirming good hope in obtaining salvation. Also Cornelius by giving alms and by praying[4] has merited being instructed by Peter, like Philip

---

[2] Found in Tertullian's largest extant work, *Adversus Marcionem* (c. 207). Cf. chapter II, footnote 1.

[3] Cf. chapter II, footnote 2.

[4] Acts 10, 4 f.

instructed the [Ethiopian] eunuch.[5] When Augustine
searched zealously for Christ in the Epistles of Paul, he
deserved finding him. Here we could state, in order to
assuage those who permit man no possibility for any good
unless indebted to God, that we owe our entire life work
to God, without whom we could accomplish nothing; furthermore, that the free will contributes very little to an
effect; finally, that it is also a work of divine grace that
we can turn our heart to the things of salvation and cooperate with grace. Augustine gained a more unfavorable
view of the free will, because of his fight with Pelagius than
he had held before. Luther, on the other hand, who at
first attributed something to the free will, has come to
deny it completely in the heat of his defense. Thus Lycurgus was criticized by the Greeks because in his hatred
of drunkenness he ordered the vines cut down,[6] whereas
by adding a little more water to the wine drunkenness
would have been avoided without losing the use of wine.

57) *Human Nature and Salvation*

In my opinion the free will could have been so defined
as to avoid overconfidence in our merits and the other
disadvantages which Luther shuns, as well as to avoid such
as we recited above, and still not lose the advantages which
Luther admires. This, it seems to me, is accomplished by
those who attribute everything to the pulling by grace
which is the first to excite our spirit, and attribute only
something to human will in its effort to continue and not
withdraw from divine grace. But since all things have three
parts, a beginning, a continuation and an end, grace is
attributed to the two extremities, and only in continuation
does the free will effect something. Two causes meet in
this same work, the grace of God and the human will, grace

---

[5]   Acts 8, 26 ff.
[6]   Lycurgus (9th century B.C.), Spartan lawgiver. Seems a confusion with Domitian. See Suetonius, *Lives of the Caesars,* Domitian, VII, 2.

being the principal cause and will a secondary, since it is impotent without the principal cause, while the latter has sufficient strength by itself. Thus, while the fire burns through its natural strength, the principal cause is still God, who acts through the fire. God alone would indeed suffice, and without Him fire could not burn. Due to this combination, man must ascribe his total salvation to divine grace, since it is very little that the free will can effect, and even that comes from divine grace which has at first created free will and then redeemed and healed it. Thus are placated, if they can be placated, those who will not tolerate that man has some good which he does not owe to God. He owes this also to God, but in another way and under another title. Just as an inheritance coming in equal share to the children, is not called a benevolence, because it belongs by common law to all. If beyond this common right a donation is made to this or that child, it is called liberality. But children owe gratitude to their parents also under the title of their inheritance.

I will try to express in parables what we have been saying. Even the healthy eye of a man does not see in the darkness, and when it is blinded, it does not see anything in light either. Thus the will can do nothing, though free, if withdrawing from grace. But the one with good eyes can close his eyes before the light and see nothing. He can also turn his eyes away. They will not see what he could have seen. The one with blind eyes owes his gratitude in the first place to God, and only then to the doctor. Before sinning our eyes were healthy. Sin has ruined them. Whoever sees, what can he pride himself in? He can impute to himself his cautious closing and turning away of the eyes.

Listen to another parable. A father raises his child, which is yet unable to walk, which has fallen and which exerts himself, and shows him an apple, placed in front of him. The boy likes to go and get it, but due to his weak bones would soon have fallen again, if the father had not supported him by his hand and guided his steps. Thus the child comes, led by the father, to the apple which the father places willingly into his hand, like a reward for his walking. The child could not have raised itself without the father's help; would not have seen the apple without the father's showing; would not have stepped forward without the father's helping his weak little steps; would not have reached the apple without the father's placing it into his hand. What can the child claim for himself? Yet, he did do something, but he must not glory in his own strength, since he owes everything to the father.

Let us assume it is the same with God. What does the child do? As the boy is being helped up, he makes an effort and tries to accommodate his weak steps to the father's guidance. The father could have pulled him against his will. A childish whim could have refused the apple. The father could have given the apple without his running, but he would rather give it in this manner, because it is better for the boy. I readily admit that our striving contributes less to the gaining of eternal life, than the boy's running at the hand of his father.

58) Criticism of Carlstadt: Grace and Freedom like Soul and Body

Here we saw how little is attributed to the freedom of the will. Nevertheless to some it still seems too much. They want only grace to act in us, and want our will only to suffer [passively], like a tool of the Divine Spirit, so that the good can, under no circumstances, be called ours, unless divine goodness imputes it to us freely. Grace is effective in us not through the free will, but within free will, just as [they say] the causality of the potter is within the clay and not through it.

Whence comes then the mention of the crown and the reward? It is said that God crowns his gifts in us, and orders that his favor be our reward. Whatever he has effected in us, he gives, in order to make us worthy of partnership in his celestial kingdom. Here I don't see how they define a free will which effects nothing. For, if they said that moved by grace it acts simultaneously, it would be easier to explain. Just as according to the natural philosophers our body obtains its first movements from the soul, without which it could not move at all, yet it not only does move, but also moves other things, and just as a partner of work participates also in its honor. If God so works in us as the potter on the clay, what good or evil could be imputed to us? For, we must not bring into this discussion the soul of Jesus Christ, who too was a tool of the Divine Spirit. And if the weakness of the body stands in the way of man meriting anything, so [Christ] before his death was terrified: he wished that not his will, but that of the Father be done.[7] And nonetheless they acknowledge this [will] to be the fountain of merit, though depriving all other saints of all the merit of their good works.

59) *Addressed to Luther*

Those who deny any freedom of the will and affirm absolute necessity, admit that God works in man not only the good works, but also evil ones. It seems to follow that inasmuch as man can never be the author of good works, he can also never be called the author of evil ones. This opinion seems obviously to attribute cruelty and injustice to God, something religious ears abhor vehemently. (He would no longer be God if anything vicious and imperfect were met in him). Nonetheless those holding such an implausible view have an answer: He is God; He is able to do only the best and most beautiful. If you observe the fittingness of the universe, even what is evil in itself, is good in it and illustrates the glory of God. No creature can adjudge the Creator's intentions. Man must subject himself completely to them. In fact, if it pleases God to damn this or that one, nobody must grumble, but accept what pleases him, and be convinced that he does everything for the best. What would come of it if man were to ask God why he did not make him an angel? Wouldn't God answer

---

[7]   Matthew 26, 39.

rightly: you impudent one! If I had made you a frog, could you then complain? The same, if the frog disputes with God: why have you not made me a peacock, conspicuous for its multicolored feathers? Would not God be justified in saying: ungrateful one! I could have made you a fungus or a bulb, but now you jump, drink and sing. Again, if a basilisk or snake were to say: why have you made me a deadly animal hated by all, and not a sheep? What would God answer? Doubtlessly he would say: I like it this way. It suits the decoration and order of the universe. You have suffered as little injury as all the flies, gnats and other insects. Each I have fashioned to appear as a miracle for him who contemplates it. And a spider, is she not a beautiful animal, even if different from the elephant? Truly, there is a greater miracle in the spider than in the elephant. Are you not satisfied in being a perfect animal in your kind? Poison was not given to you to kill others with, but to protect yourself and your little ones. Just as oxen have horns, lions have claws, wolves teeth, horses hoofs. Every animal has its utility. The horse bears burdens, the ox plows, the donkey and dog help at work, the sheep serves man for food and clothing, and you are needed for making medicine.

60) *Further Exaggeration and Difficulties*

But let us cease reasoning with those devoid of reason. We began our disputation with man, created in the image and likeness of God, and for whose pleasure He created all things. We note that some are born with healthy bodies and good minds, as though born for virtue, again others with monstrous bodies and horrible sickness, others so stupid that they almost have fallen to the level of brute animals, some even more brutish than the brutes, others so disposed toward disgraceful passions, that it seems a strong fate is impelling them, others insane and possessed by the devils. How will we explain the question of God's justice and mercy in such cases? Shall we say with Paul: "O the depth . . ." (Romans 11,33)? I think this would be better than to judge with impious rashness God's decisions, which man cannot explore. And truly, it is even more difficult to explain how God crowns his favors in some with immortal life, and punishes his misdeeds in others with eternal suffering. In order to defend such a paradox they resort to other paradoxes and to maintain the battle against their adversary. They immensely exaggerate original sin which supposedly has corrupted even the most excellent faculties of human nature, makes man incapable of anything, save only ignoring and hating God, and not even after grace and justification by faith can he effect any work which wouldn't be sin. They make that inclination to sin in us, remaining after the sin of our first parents, an invincible sin in itself, so that not one divine precept exists which even a man justified by faith could possibly keep. All the commandments of God have supposed no other purpose than to amplify the grace of God, which, irrespective of merit, grants salvation.

However, they seem to me to minimize God's mercy in one place, in order to enlarge it elsewhere, in the same manner, as one placing parsimoniously before his guests a very small breakfast, in order to make dinner appear more splendidly; or just as imitating a painter who darkens that [part of a canvas] which will be closest to the spot he wishes to be emitting the light in the picture.

At first they make God almost cruel, who, because of somebody else's sin, rages against all mankind, cruel especially since those who sinned have done penance and were punished severely as long as they lived. Secondly, when they say that even those justified by faith can do nothing but sin, so that loving and trusting God we deserve God's hatred and disfavor: doesn't this diminish divine grace that man justified by faith can still do nothing else but sin? Moreover, while God has burdened man with so many commandments which have no effect other than to make him hate God more and make his damnation more severe, does this not make God a harsher tyrant than even Dionysius of Sicily, who zealously issued many laws which, as he suspected, would not be observed by the multitude, unless strictly enforced? At first he closed his eyes to this, but soon, seeing that almost everybody transgressed in some way, began to call them to account, rendering them all punishable. And yet, God's laws were such that they could have easily been observed if only men had wanted to do so.

I do not want to investigate now, why they teach it to be impossible for us to keep all of God's commandments, for that is not our purpose here. We wish to show how they, by eagerly enlarging grace on account of salvation, have actually obscured it in others. I do not see how such [views] can endure. They liquidate the freedom of the will and teach that man is driven by the Spirit of Christ whose nature cannot bear fellowship with sin. At the same time, they say man does nothing but sin after having received grace.

Luther seems to enjoy such exaggerations. He pushes other people's exaggerations even further, driving out bad knots with worse wedges, as the saying goes. Some had daringly advanced another exaggeration, selling not only their own, but also the merits of all the saints. What kind of works [is meant]: songs, chanting the psalms, [eating of] fishes, fasting, dressing [simply], titles? Thus Luther drove one nail through with another, when he said the saints had no merits whatsoever, and that the works of even the most pious men were sin and would adduce eternal damnation if faith and divine mercy had not come to the rescue. The other side was making a considerable profit with confession and reparation. Human conscience was thereby exceedingly entangled. Likewise, all kinds of strange things were related concerning purgatory. The opponents [i.e. Luther] correct these mistakes by saying confession is the Devil's invention, and should not be required, and they think no satisfaction is necessary for sin, because Christ has atoned for the sin of all; and think there is no purgatory. One side goes so far as to say that the orders of any prior of a monastery are binding under pain of hell, while they have no scruples in promising eternal life to those who obey them. The opponents answer this exaggeration by saying that all the orders of popes, councils and bishops are heretical and anti-Christian. The one side exalts papal power in an exaggerated way, the other side speaks of the pope such that I do not dare to repeat it. Again, one side says the vows of monks and priests fetter man forever under punishment of hell, the others say such vows are godless and not to be made, and once made, to be broken.

61) *Differences between Exhortation and Doctrine*

The whole world is now shaken by the thunder and lightning born of the collision of such exaggerations. If both sides hold fast to their exaggeration, I foresee such a battle as between Achilles and Hector: since both were headstrong, only death could separate them. True, there is the popular saying, if you want to straighten a curved stick, bend it in the opposite direction. But this applies to the correction of morals. I do not know whether to employ it in matters of dogma.

In the case of exhortations and dissuasion I see sometimes a place for an exaggeration. If one wishes to encourage the timid man, one would be right in exhorting: "Don't fear, God will speak and do everything in you." And in order to dampen a man's godless insolence, you might profitably say, man can do nothing but sin; and to those who demand that their dogmas be thought equal to the canonical books say that all men are liars.

When in the investigation of truth, however, axioms are propounded, I believe one must not use paradoxes, because they are so similar to riddles. I like moderation best. Pelagius attributes much too much to the free will; Scotus attributes quite a bit. But Luther mutilates it at first by amputating its right arm. And not content with this, he has killed the freedom of the will and has removed it all together.

I like the sentiments of those who attribute a little to the freedom of the will, the most, however, to grace. One must not avoid the Scylla of arrogance by going into the Charybdis of desperation and indolence. In resetting a disjointed limb, one must not dislocate it in the opposite direction, but put it back in its place. One must not fight with an enemy in such a manner that turning the face, you are caught off guard.

According to this moderation man can do a good, albeit imperfect work; man should not boast about it; there will be some merit, but man owes it completely to God. The life of us mortals abounds in many infirmities, imperfections and vices. Whoever wishes to contemplate himself, will easily lower his head.[8] But we do not assume that even a justified man is capable of nothing but sin, especially because Christ speaks of rebirth and Paul of a new creature. • Why, you ask, is anything attributed to the freedom of the will, then? It is in order to justify blaming the godless ones who resist spitefully the grace of God; to prevent calumnies attributing cruelty and injustice to God; to prevent despair in us; to prevent a false sense of security; to stimulate our efforts. For these reasons the freedom of the will is asserted by all. Yet it is, however, ineffectual without the continuous grace of God, in order not to arrogate anything to ourselves. Someone says, what's the good of the freedom of the will, if it does not effect anything? I answer, what's the good of the entire man, if God treats him like the potter his clay, or as he can deal with a pebble?

62) *Final Conclusions*

Hence, if it has sufficiently been demonstrated, this matter is as follows: It does not promote piety to investigate this any further than must be, especially before those who are unlearned. We have proven that our opinion is more evident in scriptural testimony than the opinion of the opponents. It is a fact that Holy Scripture is in most instances either obscure and figurative, or seems, at first

---

[8] "Crista" means comb of a rooster.

sight, to contradict itself. Therefore, whether we like it or not, we sometimes had to recede from the literal meaning, and had to adjust its meaning to an interpretation. Finally, it has been plainly shown how many unreasonable, not to say absurd things follow, if we eliminate the freedom of the will. It has been made plain that the opinion, as I have been elucidating it, when accepted, does not eliminate the pious and Christian things Luther argues for—concerning the highest love of God; the rejection of exclusive faith in merits, works and our strength; the complete trust in God according to his promises. Hence, I want the reader to consider whether he thinks it is fair to condemn the opinion offered by the Church Fathers, approved for so many centuries by so many people, and to accept some paradoxes which are at present disturbing the Christian world. If the latter are true, I admit freely to my mental sloth and inability to grasp. I know for certain that I am not resisting the truth, that I love from the bottom of my heart true evangelical liberty, and that I detest everything adverse to the Gospels. Thus I am here not as a judge, as I said at the outset, but as a disputer. Nevertheless, I can truly affirm that I have served religiously in this debate, as was demanded once upon a time of judges trying matters of life and death. Though I am an old man, I'm neither ashamed nor irked to be taught by a younger if he teaches with evangelical gentleness more evident truths.

Here some will say: Erasmus should learn about Christ and disregard human prudence. This nobody understands, unless he has the Spirit of God.

Now, if I do not yet understand what Christ is, certainly we must have gone far astray from our topic and goal, though I should love nothing more than to learn which Spirit so many doctors and Christian people possessed— because it seems probable that the people believed what their bishops have already taught for thirteen centuries— who did not understand this.

I have come to the end. It is for others to judge.

Part Two

LUTHER

THE BONDAGE OF THE WILL

I

INTRODUCTION*

To THE Venerable Master Erasmus of Rotterdam, Martin Luther wishes Grace and Peace in Christ.

[600] That I have been so long in answering your Diatribe on the free will, venerable Erasmus, has happened against the expectation of all and against my usual wont, because thus far I have not only gladly embraced such opportunities for writing, but have also freely searched for them. . . I concede to you openly, a thing I have never done before, that you not only surpass me by far in literary prowess and intellectuality (which we all grant to you as your due, and the more so, since I am a barbarian occupied with the barbarous), but that you have in two ways also dampened my spirits and impetuousness, and slackened my strength before the battle began. First, because artfully you debate this matter with wonderful and continuous restraint, preventing thereby my becoming angry with you. [601] Second, because by chance or fortune or fate you say nothing on so great a subject which has not already been stated before, and you say even less, and attribute more to free will than the Sophists[1] hitherto did (I shall speak more of this later), so that it seeemed quite superfluous to answer your invalid arguments.

I have already often refuted them myself. And Philip

---

* Cf. W.A. 600-602. This is the standard reference to the Weimar edition, *Weimarer Ausgabe,* of Luther's works.
[1] Luther calls the Scholastics such, because he condemns their theology as sophistry.

Melanchthon has trampled them underfoot in his unsurpassed book *Concerning Theological Questions.*[2] His is a book which, in my judgment, deserves not only being immortalized, but also being included in the Church's canon, in comparison with which your book is, in my opinion, so contemptible and worthless that I feel great pity for you for having defiled your beautiful and skilled manner of speaking with such vile dirt. . . To those who have drunk of the teaching of the Spirit in my books, we have given in abundance and more than enough, and they easily despise your arguments. But it is not surprising that those reading without the Spirit are tossed like a reed with every wind. . . . Hence, you see, I lost all desire to answer you, not because I was busy, or because it would have been a difficult task, nor on account of your great eloquence, nor for fear of you, but simply because of disgust, indignation and contempt, which, if I say so, expresses my judgment of your Diatribe. . . [602] If I do answer, it is because faithful brethren in Christ press me to it. . . And who knows but that God may even condescend to visit you, dearest Erasmus, through me, His poor weak vessel, and that I may (which from my heart I desire of the Father of mercies through Jesus Christ our Lord) come to you in this book in a happy hour and gain a dearest brother. For although you write wrongly concerning free will, I owe you no small thanks, because you have confirmed my own view. Seeing the case for free will argued with such great talents, yet leaving it worse than it was before, is an evident proof that free will is a downright lie. It is like the woman of the gospel: the more the physicians treat her case, the worse it gets.[3]

Therefore I shall be even more grateful if you gain greater certainty through me, just as I have gained in assurance through you. But both are the gift of the Spirit, and not the work of our own endeavors. So we should pray to

---

2   *Loci Theologici,* 1521
3   Cf. Luke 8, 43 and Mark 5, 26

God that He will open my mouth, and your and all men's hearts: that He may be the teacher in the midst of us, who may in us speak and hear.

My friend Erasmus, may I ask you to suffer my lack of eloquence, as I in return will bear with your ignorance in these matters. God does not give everything to each and we cannot all do everything. As Paul says, "Now there are varieties of gifts, but the same Spirit" (1 Corinthians 12,4). It remains, therefore, that these gifts render a mutual service. One with his gift bear the burden of the other's lack. Thus we shall fulfill the law of Christ.[4]

---

[4] Cf. Galatians 6, 2

II

REFUTATION OF ERASMUS' PREFACE *

(Erasmus 2 & 3)
Assertions in Christianity

To begin with, I would like to review some parts of your Preface in which you attempt to disparage our case and to embellish your own.

First, I notice that, as in your other works, you censure me for obstinacy of assertion. Here in this book you say your "dislike of assertions is so great that you prefer the views of the sceptics wherever the inviolable authority of Scripture and the decisions of the Church permit; though you gladly submit your opinion whether you comprehend what she prescribes or not." Such outlook appeals to you. [603] I assume (in courtesy bound) that you say these things from your charitable mind and love of peace. If, however, another had said it, I should, perhaps, have attacked him in my usual way. And even you, well-meaning as you are, I ought not to allow to err in this matter. Not to delight in assertions is not the mark of a Christian heart. Indeed, one must delight in assertions to be a Christian at all! To avoid misunderstandings, let me define *assertion*. I mean a constant adhering to and affirming of your position, avowing and defending it, and invincibly persevering in

* W.A. 603-639

it. . . . Far be it from us Christians to be sceptics and academics![5]

Let there be men who assert twice as determined as the very Stoics themselves! I pray you, how often does the Apostle Paul require that assurance of faith, that is, a most certain and firm assertion of conscience. In Romans 10,10 he calls it confession, "and with the mouth profession of faith is made unto salvation." And Christ says, "Therefore, everyone who acknowledges me before me, I also will acknowledge him before my Father in heaven" (Matthew 10,32). Peter commands us to give a reason of the hope that is in us.[6]

But what's the need for so many proofs? Nothing is more known and characteristic among Christians than assertions. Take away assertions and you take away Christianity. Indeed, the Holy Spirit is given to Christians from heaven, so that He may in them glorify Christ and confess Him even unto death. And to die for what you confess and assert is not an assertion? What a clown I would hold a man to be who does not really believe, nor unwaveringly assert the things he is reproving others with! Why, I would send him to Anticyra![7]

[604] But I am the biggest fool, losing words and time on something clearer than the sun. What Christian can bear that assertions should be deprecated? That would be to deny at once all piety and religion, like asserting that piety, religion and all dogmas are nothing at all. Why do *you assert* your "dislike of assertions" and your preferring an open mind?

---

[5] See Erasmus, section 2, on scepticism. Academics refers in general to the "intellectuals," and in particular to the Platonists, the generations of members of the Academy. Sceptics were members of the so-called Middle and New Academy.

[6] 1 Peter 3, 15, "Be ready always with an answer to everyone who asks a reason for the hope that is in you."

[7] Anticyra, a name of three Grecian health resorts in Thessaly, Phocis and Locris, famous for the hellebore which grew there and which was in high repute as a medicine to clear the brain and cure stupidity.

But you remind me, and rightly so, that you were not referring to confessing Christ and His doctrines. And in courtesy to you, I give up the right of which I normally avail myself and refrain from judging your heart. I leave this for another time, or to other writers. In the meantime, I admonish you to correct your tongue and your pen, and to refrain henceforth from using such expressions. However upright and honest your heart may be, your words, which are the index of the heart, they say, are not so. . . .

No Liberty to Be a Sceptic

. . . What a Proteus[8] is the man talking about "inviolable authority of Scriptures and the decisions of the Church"! —as if you had the greatest respect for the Scriptures and the Church, when in the same breath you explain that you wish you had the liberty to be a sceptic! What Christian could talk like this? . . . A Christian will rather say this: I am so against the sentiments of sceptics that, so far as the weakness of the flesh permits, I shall not only steadfastly adhere to the sacred writings everywheres, and in all parts of them, and assert them, but also I wish to be as positive as possible on nonessentials that lie outside Scriptures, because what is more miserable, than uncertainty. . . . [605] . . . In short, your words amount to this, that it matters little to you what anyone believes anywheres, as long as the peace of the world is undisturbed. . . You seem to look upon the Christian doctrines as nothing better than the opinions of philosophers and men. Of course, it is stupid to wrangle and quarrel over these, as nothing results but contention and disturbance of the public peace. . . So you wish to end *our* fighting as an intermediate peacemaker. . . Allow *us* to be assertors. You go ahead and favor your sceptics and academics, till

---

[8]   Allusion to Proteus, "the old man of the sea" of Greek mythology, refers to his power of assuming many different shapes and forms; being changeable.

Christ calls you too! The Holy Spirit is no sceptic, and what He has written into our hearts are no doubts or opinions, but assertions, more certain and more firm than all human experience and life itself.

(Erasmus 4)
Clarity of Scriptures

[606]. . . I hope you credit Luther with some acquaintance with and judgment in the sacred writings. If not, beware and I'll wring the admission from you! This is the distinction which I make (for I too am going to act a little the rhetorician and logician): God and the Scriptures are two things, just like God and creation are two things. Nobody doubts that in God many things are hidden of which we know nothing. . . But that there are in Scriptures some things abstruse and not quite plain, was spread by the godless Sophists, whom you echo, Erasmus. They have never yet produced one article to prove this their madness. Satan has frightened men from reading the sacred writings, and has rendered Holy Scriptures contemptible, so as to ensure his poisonous philosophy to prevail in the church. I admit that many passages in Scriptures are obscure and abstruse. But that is due to our ignorance of certain terms and grammatical particulars, and not to the majesty of the subject. This ignorance does not in any way prevent our knowing all the contents of Scriptures. What things can Scriptures still be concealing, now that the seals are broken, the stone rolled from the door of the sepulchre, and that greatest of all mysteries brought to light: Christ became man; God is Trinity and Unity; Christ suffered for us and will reign forever? Are not these things known and proclaimed even in our streets? Take Christ out of Scriptures and what will you find remaining in them? All the things contained in the Scriptures, therefore, are made manifest (even though some passages containing unknown words are yet obscure). But it is absurd and impious to

say that things are obscure, because of a few obscure words, when you know the contents of Scriptures being set in the clearest light. And if the words are obscure in one place, yet they are clear in another. . .

(Erasmus 5 & 6)
The Crucial Issue: Knowing Free Will

[609]. . . You draft for us a list of those things which you consider sufficient for Christian piety. Any Jew or Gentile utterly ignorant of Christ could easily draw up the same, because you do not mention Christ in a single letter. As though you thought that Christian piety is possible without Christ, if God be but worshipped with one's whole heart as being a "naturally most benign God." What shall I say here, Erasmus? You ooze Lucian from every pore; you swill Epicurus by the gallons.[9] If you consider this subject not necessary to Christians, I ask you to withdraw from the debate. We have no common ground. I consider it vital.

[610] If, as you say, it be irreligious, curious, superfluous to know whether God's foreknowledge is contingent; whether our will can contribute anything pertinent to our eternal salvation, or whether it simply endures operative grace; whether everything we do, good or evil, is done out of mere necessity, or whether we are rather enduring, what then, I ask, is religious, serious and useful knowledge? This is weak stuff, Erasmus. *Das ist zu viel!*[10]

It is difficult to attribute this to your ignorance, because

[9]   Lucian, 2nd century A.D. Greek author, born in Syria, died in Egypt. He is famous for his many rhetorical and satirical narratives, mostly in dialogue form. His reputation was that of one of the wittiest ancients. He ridiculed the Christian religion.—Epicurus, 3rd century B.C. Greek teacher and founder of Epicureanism, born in Samos, died in Athens. He regarded belief in supernaturalism as a superstition and denied the existence of providential gods.

[10]   Luther has become so upset in quoting the above from Erasmus that he exclaims in German, "that's too much," in the midst of his Latin.

you are now old, you have lived among Christians and you have long been studying the sacred writings. You leave me no room for excusing or thinking well of you. And yet the Papists pardon and put up with these outrageous statements, because you are writing against Luther. Without a Luther in the case, they would tear you apart. Here I must speak like Aristotle when arguing with his master Plato: Plato is my friend, but truth must be honored above all. Granted you have but little understanding of Scripture and Christian piety, surely even an enemy of Christians ought to know what Christians do, consider useful and necessary. But you, a theologian and teacher of Christianity, wanting to write an outline guide for Christianity, forget your own sceptical way. Otherwise you would vacillate as to what is profitable and necessary for Christians. In fact, you defy your own principles and make an unheard of assertion that here is something nonessential. If it is really unessential, and not surely known, then neither God, Christ, the gospel, faith nor anything else even of Judaism, let alone Christianity, is left. In the name of the immortal God, Erasmus, how wide a window, how big a field are you opening up for attack against you.

. . . [611] . . . The essence of Christianity which you describe. . . is without Christ, without the Spirit, and chillier than ice. . . You plainly assert that the will is effective in things pertaining to eternal salvation, when you speak of its striving. And again you assert that it is passive, when saying that without the mercy of God it is ineffective. But you fail to define the limits within which we should think of the will as acting and as being acted upon. Thus you keep us in ignorance as to how far the mercy of God extends, and how far our own will extends; what man's will and God's mercy really *do* effect. That prudence of yours carries you along. You side with neither party and escape safely through Scylla and Charybdis, in order that coming into open sea, overwhelmed and confounded by the waves, you can then assert all that you now deny, and deny all that you now assert! . . .

. . . [613] It is not irreligious, curious or superfluous, but extremely wholesome and necessary for a Christian to know whether or not his will has anything to do in matters pertaining to salvation. This, let me tell you, is the very hinge upon which our disputation turns. It is the crucial issue between you and me. It is our aim to inquire what free will can do, in what it is passive, and how it is related to the grace of God. If we know nothing of these things, we shall know nothing whatsoever of Christianity, and shall be worse off than all the heathens. Whoever does not understand this, let him confess that he is not a Christian. But he who derides and ridicules it, should know that he is the greatest foe of Christians. . . It is necessary to distinguish most clearly between the power of God and our own, between God's works and ours, if we are to live a godly life.

Foreknowledge of God

. . . [615] . . . In this book, therefore, I shall harry you and all the Sophists until you shall define for me the power of free will. And I hope so to harry you (Christ helping me) as to make you heartily repent ever having published your Diatribe. It is then essentially necessary and wholesome for Christians to know that God foreknows nothing contingently, but that he foresees, purposes and does all things according to His immutable, eternal and infallible will. This thunderbolt throws free will flat and utterly dashes it to pieces. Those who want to assert it must either deny this thunderbolt or pretend not to see it. . .

Tyranny of Laws

. . . [624] . . . In the remaining example concerning confession and satisfaction, it is wonderful to observe with what dexterous prudence you proceed. . . You denounce the common people, because in their depravity they abuse the preaching of freedom from confession and satisfaction for their own carnal liberty. And now you say that the necessity of making confession restrains them to some extent. . . Why, with this reasoning you bring upon us the universal tyranny of the Papal laws, as useful and wholesome; because by them also the depravity of the common people is restrained. I shall not inveigh against this passage, as it deserves. I'll just state briefly: a good theologian teaches that the common people should be restrained by the external power of the sword when they do evil, as Paul teaches (Romans 13,1-4). But their conscience must not be fettered by false laws, and thereby be tormented for sins there where God had willed to be no sins at all. For consciences are bound by the law of God alone. So that Papal tyranny, which falsely terrifies and murders the souls within, and uselessly exhausts the bodies without, is to be banished forthwith. Although it binds men to confession and other burdens by external pressure, it fails to restrain their minds, which are only the more provoked into the hatred of both God and men. Such external butchery of the body is in vain. It just makes for hypocrites. So that tyrants, with such laws, are nothing but raving wolves, robbers and plunderers of souls. And now you, an excellent counselor of souls, recommend to us once more these barbarous soul-murderers, who fill the world with blaspheming, vain hypocrites solely in order to restrain them a little from outward sin. . .

(Erasmus 7)

The Christian's Peace

. . . [625] . . . You make it clear that this peace and tranquility of the flesh are to you far more important than faith, conscience, salvation, the word of God, the glory of Christ and God himself. Therefore, let me tell you, and I beg you to let it sink deep into your mind, I am concerned

with a serious, vital and eternal verity, yes such a funda-
mental one, that it ought to be maintained and defended
at the cost of life itself, and even though the whole world
should not only be thrown into turmoil and fighting, but
shattered in chaos and reduced to nothing. If you don't
grasp this, or if you are not moved by this, then mind your
own business, and leave us to whom God has given it to
grasp and to be affected by it. . .

[626] May Christ grant, I for one desire and hope so,
that your heart may not be, as your words certainly imply,
in agreement with Epicurus, considering the word of God
and the future life to be mere stories. . . It is constantly
the case with the word of God that because of it, the world
is thrown into confusion. Christ openly declares: "I come
not to send peace but a sword" (Matthew 10,34). And in
Luke: "I come to send fire upon the earth" (Luke 12,49);
so in Paul, "in tumults" (2 Corinthians 6,5) etc. . . . The
world and its god[11] cannot and will not bear the word of
the true God. And the true God cannot and will not keep
silence. Since these two gods are at war with each other,
how can there be anything else throughout the whole world,
but uproar?

Therefore, to wish to silence this turmoil is really to
want to hinder the word of God and stop its course. For
wherever it comes, the word of God comes to change and
renew the world. . . It is the Christian's part to expect
and endure these things. . . I see indeed, my dear Erasmus,
that you deplore the loss of peace and concord in many of
your books. . . But I am sorry that I find it necessary to
teach so great a theologian as yourself these things like a
schoolboy, when you ought to be a teacher of others. . .

Christian Liberty

. . . [627] . . . The doctrine that confession and satisfaction ought to be free, you either deny, or you do not know

---

[11]   Cf. 2 Corinthians 4, 4.

that there exists a word of God. I for my part know for sure
that there is a word of God which asserts Christian liberty,
in order that we may not be ensnared into bondage by
human traditions and human laws. . . The prince of this
world does not allow that the laws of the Popes and his
bishops be kept in liberty. His intention is to entangle and
bind consciences. This the true God will not bear. Therefore, the word of God and the traditions of men oppose each
other in irreconcilable discord. . .

[628] And as to your fear that many depraved persons
will abuse this liberty, this must be considered among those
turmoils, as part of that temporal leprosy which we must
bear, and the evil we must endure. . . You are ridiculous
enough to misquote Paul.[12] But Paul does not speak of
teaching or of teaching doctrinal truth, as you confound his
words and twist their meaning to please you. On the contrary, he would have the truth spoken everywhere, at all
times, and in every way. He is even delighted when Christ
is preached out of envy and hatred, and plainly says so.[13]
"Provided only that in every way, whether in pretense or in
truth, Christ is being proclaimed" . . . Truth and doctrine
should always be preached openly and firmly, without com-
promise or concealment . . .

. . . [629] . . . If we ask you to determine for us when,
to whom, and how truth is to be spoken, could you give an
answer? . . . Perhaps you have in mind to teach the truth
so that the Pope does not object, Caesar is not enraged,
bishops and princes are not upset, and furthermore no
uproar and turmoil are caused in the wide world, lest many
be offended and grow worse? . . . His Gospel which all need
should not be confined to any place or time. It should be
preached to all men, at all times and in all places. I have
already proved above that what is written in Scriptures is
plain to all, and is wholesome, and must be proclaimed

[12]   1 Corinthians 6, 12, "All things are lawful for me, but not all
things are expedient."
[13]   Philippians 1, 18.

abroad, as you wrote yourself in your *Paraclesis*[14] with much more wisdom then than now. Those who are unwilling for souls to be redeemed, like the Pope and his adherents, let it be left to them to bind the word of God and keep men from life and the kingdom of heaven. . . . [630] With the same prudence you advise that wrong decisions made in councils should not be openly acknowledged, lest ground for denying the authority of the fathers be thus afforded. This is indeed just what the Pope wanted you to say! And he hears it with greater pleasure than the Gospel itself. He will be most ungrateful, if he does not honor you in return with a cardinal's cap, together with all the revenues belonging to it . . . I must tell you again: men's ordinances cannot be observed together with the word of God, because the former bind consciences and the latter looses them. . . . The authority of the Fathers is therefore nothing . . . for Christ is a higher authority.

Spontaneity of Necessitated Acts

[632] You say: Who will endeavor to reform his life? I answer: Nobody! No man can! God has no time for your self-reformers, for they are hypocrites. The elect who fear God will be reformed by the Holy Spirit. The rest will perish unreformed. Note how Augustine does not say that the works of none or of all are crowned, but that the works of some are. "Therefore there will be some who reform their lives."

You say, by our doctrine a floodgate of iniquity is opened. Be it so. Ungodly men are part of that evil leprosy spoken of before. Nevertheless, these are the same doctrines which throw open to the elect, who fear God, a gateway to righteousness, an entrance into heaven, a way unto God . . . These truths are published for the sake of the elect, that they may be humbled and brought down to nothing and so

---

[14] A book published in 1516 in which Erasmus pleads for the study of Christian philosophy.

be saved. The rest resist this humiliation. They condemn the teaching of self-desperation. They wish to have left a little something that they may do themselves. Secretly they continue proud, and enemies of the grace of God.

. . . [634] . . . As to the other paradox you mention, that whatever is done by us, is not done by free will, but of mere necessity, let us briefly consider it, lest we should let such a pernicious remark go unchallenged. I observe: if it be proved that our salvation is not of our own strength or counsel, but depends on the working of God alone (which I hope I shall clearly prove later in the main discussion), does it not evidently follow that when God is not present to work in us, everything we do is evil, and that we of necessity act in a way not availing unto our salvation? For if it is not we ourselves, but God only, who works salvation in us, it follows that nothing we do before His working in us avails unto salvation. By necessity I do not mean compulsion. I meant what they term the necessity of immutability. That is to say, a man void of the Spirit of God does not do evil against his will, under pressure, as though taken by the neck and forced into it, . . . but he does it spontaneously and willingly. And this willingness and desire of doing evil he cannot, by his own strength, eliminate, restrain or change. He goes on still desiring and craving to do evil. And if external pressure compels him to act outwardly to the contrary, yet the will within remains averse and chafes under such constraint. But it would not thus rise in indignation, if it were changed, and made willing to yield to a constraining power. This is what we mean by the necessity of immutability: that the will cannot change itself, nor give itself another bent, but, rather, the more it is resisted, the more it is irritated to crave, as its indignation proves. This would not be the case if it were free or had a free will. . . .

. . . [635] On the other hand, when God works in us, the will is changed under the sweet influence of the Spirit of God. It desires and acts not from compulsion, but responsively of its own desire and inclination. It cannot be

altered by any opposition. It cannot be compelled or overcome even by the gates of hell. It still goes on to desire,
crave after and love that which is good, just as once it
desired, craved after and loved evil . . . Thus the human
will is like a beast of burden. If God rides it, it wills and
goes whence God wills; as the Psalm says, "I was as a beast
of burden before thee" (Psalm 72,22). If Satan rides, it
wills and goes where Satan wills. Nor may it choose to
which rider it will run, nor which it will seek. But the riders
themselves contend who shall have and hold it.

Grace and Free Will

. . . [636] And now, what if I prove from your own
words, in which you assert the freedom of the will, that
there is no such thing as free will at all? What, if I should
show that you unwittingly deny what you labor with so
much sagacity to affirm? If I fail here, I promise to revoke
all that I wrote against you in this book; and all that your
Diatribe advances against me shall be confirmed!

You make the power of free will small and utterly ineffective apart from the grace of God.[15] Acknowledged?
Now then, I ask you: If God's grace is wanting, or if it be
taken away from that certain small degree of power, what
can it do for itself? You say it is ineffective and can do
nothing good. Therefore it will not do what God or His
grace wills. And why? Because we have now taken God's
grace away from it, and what the grace of God does not do
is not good. Hence it follows that free will without the grace
of God is not free at all, but is the permanent bond-slave
and servant of evil, since it cannot turn itself unto good.
This being determined, I allow you to enlarge the power of
free will as much as you like, make it angelic, divine, if you
can. But once you add this doleful postscript, that it is

---

[15] Luther may here be referring to sections 15, 16 or 20 in
Erasmus.

ineffective apart from God's grace, you at once rob it of all its power. What is ineffective power, but plainly no power at all. Therefore, to say that free will exists and has power, though ineffective, is, what the Sophists call a contradiction in terms. It is like saying, free will is something which is not free.

... [638] But, if we do not want to drop this term altogether (which would be the safest and most Christian thing to do), we may still use it in good faith denoting free will in respect not of what is above him, but of what is below him. This is to say, man should know in regard to his goods and possessions the right to use them, to do or to leave undone, according to his free will. Although at the same time, that same free will is overruled by the free will of God alone, just as He pleases. However, with regard to God, and in all things pertaining to salvation or damnation, man has no free will, but is a captive, servant and bond-slave, either to the will of God, or to the will of Satan.

Summary of Preface

These observations on the heads of your Preface embrace nearly the entire subject under debate, almost more so than the following body of the book. The essence of it all could have been summed up in the following "dilemma": [16] Your Preface complains either of the words of God or of the words of men. If the latter, it is all written in vain. If the former, it is all blasphemy. Wherefore it would have saved much trouble, if it had been plainly mentioned whether we were disputing concerning the words of God, or the words of men. But this will, perhaps, be handled in your Introduction which follows, or in the body of the work itself ... We teach nothing save Christ crucified. But Christ crucified brings all these doctrines along with Himself, including

---

[16]   Luther uses "dilemma" in an original sense of a syllogistic argument which presents an antagonist with two (or more) alternatives, equally conclusive against him, whichever alternate is chosen.

"wisdom also among those that are perfect." No other wisdom may be taught among Christians than that which is "hidden in a mystery," and this belongs only to the "perfect"— and not to the sons of a Judaizing, legal-minded generation, who, without faith, boast of their works!

III

REFUTATION
OF ERASMUS' INTRODUCTION *

(Erasmus 8)
Denying Church Fathers' Authority

[639] . . . At the beginning of our disputation proper you promised to argue according to the canonical books, "since Luther recognizes no [extracanonical] authority." [640] Very well! I welcome your promise . . . You tell us that you are much influenced by so great a number of the most learned men . . . Biblical scholars, holy martyrs, many renowned for miracles, together with the more recent theologians, many schools, councils, bishops and popes. In a word, on your side, you say, is learning, ability, numbers, greatness, courage, holiness, miracles, while on my side there are only Wycliffe and Lorenzo Valla . . . [642] But tell me this: was anyone of them made a saint, did anyone of them receive the Spirit or work miracles in the name of the free will, or by the power of the free will, or to confirm the free will? Far from it, you will say, but in the name and by the power of Jesus Christ were all those things done, and for the confirmation of the doctrine of Christ . . . Wherefore your appeal to the holiness, the Spirit and the miracles of the Fathers is pointless. These do not prove the free will,

---

* W.A. 639-661

but the doctrine of Jesus Christ which contradicts free will . . . [649] . . . Those who assert the free will . . . in blindness and ignorance, pick that which the Fathers, stumbling in the weakness of their flesh have said in favor of free will, and oppose it to that which the same Fathers, in the power of the Spirit, have elsewhere said against free will. . . . So did that disgusting Faber of Constance.[17]

(Erasmus 9-12)
Invisible Church and Clarity of Scriptures

. . . [650] . . . The Creed which we all hold runs thus, "I believe in the holy catholic Church" . . . [651] . . . Show me under the kingdom of the Pope one single bishop discharging his office. Show me a single council at which they dealt with matters of religion, and not with gowns, dignities, revenues and other profanities, which only the mad could consider pertaining to the Holy Spirit! Nevertheless they are called the Church . . . And yet even under them Christ has preserved His Church, though it is not called the church. How many saints do you imagine the inquisition having burned and killed, such as John Hus?[18] No doubt, many holy men of the same spirit lived in those times.

Why don't you rather marvel at this, Erasmus, that in general there were, from the beginning of time, superior talents, greater learning a more ardent pursuit among pagans than among Christians and the people of God? As Christ Himself declares, "The children of this world . . . are more prudent than the children of light" (Luke 16,8) . . . [652] . . . Therefore, what shall we do? The Church is

---

[17] Johannes Faber, suffragan bishop of Constance had just (1524) published his *Malleus in Haeresin Lutheranam.*
[18] Bohemian religious reformer (1369-1415). Acquainted with Wycliffe's teachings, he wrote against transsubstantiation, papal primacy, etc. and made Scriptures the sole rule in religious matters. He was sentenced to death by the Council of Constance and burned at the stake July 6, 1415.

hidden, the saints are unknown. What and whom shall we believe? . . . [654] . . . Scriptures, [because] they are called a way and a path, doubtless because of their perfect certainty . . . [656] . . . Wherefore, if the doctrine of free will is obscure and ambiguous it is no concern of Christians and the Scriptures, and should therefore be left alone . . . But if it does concern Christians and Scriptures, it ought to be clear, open and manifest, just like all the other articles of faith which are quite evident. For all the articles held by Christians should be most evident to themselves and also supported against adversaries by such plain and manifest scriptures as to stop all their mouths, so that they can make no reply . . . [659] . . . But why need enlarge? Why not conclude the dicussion with this your Introduction and give my verdict against you in your own words, according to Christ's saying, "by thy words thou wilt be justified, and by thy words thou wilt be condemned"? (Matthew 12,37). For you say that Scriptures are not clear upon this point. And then suspending all judgment, you discuss throughout your book only the pros and cons on each side! That's why you wish to call it a Diatribe, i.e., discussion, rather than an Apophasis, i.e., denial . . .

Luther's Conclusion

. . . [661] . . . So I conclude this small part of the Disputation. By Scriptures being obscure, nothing certain ever has been or could be defined concerning free will. This is according to your own testimony. In the lives of all the men from the beginning of the world, nothing has ever been disclosed to favor free will. I have proved that above. To teach something that is neither described by one word within Scripture, nor evinced by a single fact outside Scripture, is inappropriate for Christian doctrine, though appropriate for the very fables of Lucian. . .

Division of Luther's Work

. . . Thus I might here have concluded the whole of this free will discussion. Even the testimony of my adversaries is for me and against themselves . . . But as Paul commands us to stop the mouths of vain talkers,[19] let us now proceed to the disputation proper, handling the subject in the order in which the Diatribe proceeds: we will first confute the arguments which are brought forward in support of free will; secondly, we shall defend our own arguments that are being attacked; finally, we shall contend for the grace of God against free will.

---

[19]   Cf. Titus 1, 11.

IV

REFUTATION
OF ERASMUS' OLD AND NEW
TESTAMENT PROOFS
SUPPORTING THE FREE WILL*

(Erasmus 13)
Refuting Erasmus' Definition of Free Will

[662] Let us first of all, as is proper, begin with your definition of free will: "Under free will we understand in this
connection the ability of the human will whereby man can
turn toward or turn away from that which leads unto
eternal salvation."

Shrewdly you have stated a bare definition, without
explaining any of its parts (as others do). Perhaps you
feared more shipwrecks than one. I am therefore forced to
investigate the several parts myself. Upon closer examination the thing defined is undoubtedly of a greater extent
than the definition. The Sophists call such a definition
vicious, i.e., when a definition fails to cover fully the thing
defined. For I have shown above that free will belongs to
none but God alone. You are perhaps right in assigning to
man a will of some sort, but to credit him with free will
in the things of God is going too far. For the term free will
means in its proper sense for everybody a will that can and
does do God-ward whatever it pleases, restrained by no law
and no command . . . Here then at the outset, the definition

---

* W.A. 661-699

of the term and the definition of the thing are at odds. The term signifies one thing and what is really meant is another. It would indeed be more correct to call it "vertible-will" or "mutable-will." In this way Augustine and after him the Sophists diminished the glory and force of the term free, adding this limitation, called "vertibility of free will" . . . The clear parts of the definition then are these: "the ability of the human will," "whereby a man can," and "unto eternal salvation." But the following are blind gladiators:[20] "turn toward," "that which leads," and "turn away" . . . [663] I suppose, then that this "ability of the human will" means a power, or faculty, or disposition, or aptitude to will or not to will, to choose or refuse, to approve or disapprove, and to perform what other actions belong to the will. Now, what it means for the same power to "turn toward" or to "turn away," I do not see, unless it be the very willing or not willing, choosing or refusing, approving or disapproving, that is, the very action of the will itself. Thus we must suppose that this power is a kind of something that comes between the will and the action itself, something by which the will itself elicits the action of willing or not willing, or by which the action itself of willing or not willing is elicited. It is impossible to imagine or conceive of anything else. If I am mistaken, blame the author who gave the definition, and not me who examines it. For it is justly said among lawyers, "The words of one speaking obscurely, when he can speak more plainly, should be interpreted against him." And here I don't want to hear anything about our modern theologians[21] and their subtleties. For the sake of understanding and teaching, we must state matters very plainly. And as to those words, "which lead unto eternal salvation," I suppose they mean the words

---

[20] Luther uses here a Latin term "Andabatae," denoting gladiators who fight blindfolded. Just as ineffective are the enumerated parts of the definition.

[21] "Modernos" refers to the Nominalist branch of Scholasticism. They taught the "via moderna." Luther received much of his education from Nominalists.

and works of God, which are offered to the human will that it might apply itself to or turn away from them. I call both the law and the gospel the "words of God." The law requires works, the gospel faith. There is nothing else that leads to the grace of God, or unto eternal salvation, but the word and the work of God, because grace, or the Spirit is the very life to which the words and work of God lead us.

But this life or salvation is an eternal matter, incomprehensible to the human capacity, as Paul shows, out of Isaiah in 1 Corinthians 2,9. "Eye has not seen or ear heard, nor has it entered into the heart of man, what things God has prepared for those who love him."

. . . [664] Upon the authority of Erasmus then, free will is a power of the human will which can of itself will and not will the word and work of God, by which it is to be led to those things which are beyond its capacity and comprehension. If it can will and not will, it can also love and hate. If it can love and hate, it can, to a degree, keep the law and believe the gospel. For it is impossible, if you can will and not will, that you should not be able by that will to begin some kind of work, even though another should hinder you from completing it. And therefore since death, the cross and all the evils of the world are numbered among the works of God that lead to salvation, the human will can will its own death and perdition. Yes, it can will all things when it can will the contents of the words and works of God. What can there be anywhere below, above, within or without the word and work of God, but God Himself? But what is here then left to grace and the Holy Spirit? This is plainly to ascribe divinity to free will! For to will to embrace the law and the gospel, not to will sin, and to will death, belongs to the power of God alone, as Paul testifies in more places than one.

This means that no one since the Pelagians has written of free will more correctly than Erasmus. For I have said above that free will is a divine term and signifies a divine power. So far only the Pelagians have ever assigned to it such power. The Sophists, whatever their views, don't claim anything like this. Erasmus by far outstrips the Pelagians, for they assign this divinity to the whole free will, while Erasmus assigns it to half only. The Pelagians divide free will into two parts, the power of discernment and the power of choice, attributing the one to reason, and the other to will. The Sophists do the same. But Erasmus, setting aside the power of discernment, exalts the power of choice alone. Thus he makes a lame half free will into a god. What do you suppose he would have done, had he set out describing the whole of free will?

. . . [665] Do you see, my friend Erasmus, that by this definition you betray, unwittingly, I presume, that you know nothing at all of these matters, or that you write thoughtlessly upon the subject, knowing neither what you say nor what you affirm? As I said before, you say less about and attribute more to free will than all the rest. You fail to describe the whole free will, and yet you assign to it all things. The Sophists, or at least their father Peter Lombard[22] presents a much more tolerable view. He says that free will is the faculty of discerning, and the choosing good, if grace is with it, but evil, if grace be wanting. He plainly agrees with Augustine that free will of its own power cannot do anything but fall, nor avail unto anything but to sin. Accordingly, Augustine in his second book against Julian calls it a slave will rather than a free will.

(Erasmus 17-21)
Erasmus' Three Views on Free Will

[667] Then you invent a fourfold grace, so as to assign a sort of faith and charity even to the philosophers. And with this [you also invent] a threefold law, of nature, of

---

[22]   Peter Lombard was a 12th century scholar and traditionally the first doctor of the University of Paris. From 1159 he was also bishop of Paris. As a teacher of theology he wrote *Sententiarum Libri Quatuor,* which gave him the surname Master of Sentences. Luther, too, was trained by this classical scriptural commentary.

works, and of faith, so as to assert boldly that the precepts
of the philosophers agree with the precepts of the gospel . . .
Out of one opinion concerning free will you make three.
The first opinion, of those who deny that man can will good
without special grace, who deny that it can make progress,
perfect, etc., seems to you severe, though very probable.
And this you approve, because it leaves to man desire and
effort, but does not leave anything that he may ascribe to
his own power. The second opinion, of those who contend
that free will avails for nothing but sinning and that grace
alone works good in us, etc., seems to you more severe still.
And the third opinion, of those who say that free will is an
empty phrase, and God works in us both good and evil, and
all that comes to pass is of mere necessity, seems to you
most severe. You profess to be writing against those last
two.

Do you know what you are saying, friend Erasmus? You
are here presenting three opinions, as if belonging to three
different sects, simply because you fail to realize that it is
the same subject, stated by us, spokesmen of the same party,
only in different ways and words. Let me show you your
carelessness and sleepy stupidity of your own judgment.

I ask you, how does your previous definition of free will
square with this first opinion which you confess to be very
probable? For you said that free will is a power of the
human will by which a man can turn towards good,
whereas here you say approvingly that man without grace
cannot will good. The definition affirms what its example
denies. Hence there are found in your free will a yes and a
no. In one and the same doctrine and article in the same
breath you approve and condemn us; approve and condemn yourself. [668] Do you believe that to apply itself
to what pertains unto eternal salvation, a power your definition assigns to free will, is not good? If there is so much
good in free will that it could apply itself unto good, it
would have no need of grace. Therefore, the free will which
you define is one, and the free will you defend is another.

Erasmus, outstripping others, has now two free wills, and they militate against each other.

But setting aside the free will which the definition defines, let us consider the opposite one which this opinion proposes. You grant that man without special grace cannot will good (for we are not now discussing what the grace of God can do, but what man can do without grace); you grant then that free will cannot will good. This is nothing else but granting that it cannot apply itself to what pertains unto eternal salvation, which was the essence of your definition. Furthermore, a little earlier, you stated that the human will after sin is so depraved that it has lost its liberty and is compelled to serve sin, and cannot recall itself to a better state. And if I am not mistaken, you make the Pelagians to be of this opinion. Now here, I believe, my Proteus has no way to escape. He is caught and held fast by his own plain words: that the will having lost its liberty is tied and bound in slavery to sin. Oh noble free will! which having lost its liberty, is declared by Erasmus himself to be the slave of sin! Yet, when Luther asserted this, nothing so absurd was ever heard of! Nothing was more useless than the proclaiming of this paradox. So much so, that even the Diatribe had to be written against him! . . .

. . . [669] But perhaps this is the dream of the Diatribe that between these two, the "ability to will good" and the "inability to will good," there may be a middle ground, i.e., to will is absolute, without respect to good and evil. So that by a logical subtlety we may steer clear of the rocks and say that in the will of man there is a certain willing which indeed cannot will good without grace, but which nevertheless does not forthwith will only evil. It is a sort of mere abstract willing, pure and simple, either upward unto God by grace, or downwards unto evil by sin. But then what becomes of your statement that when it has lost its liberty it is compelled to serve sin? Where then is that desire and effort that you left it? Where is its power to apply itself to that which pertains to eternal salvation? For that power of applying itself unto salvation cannot be a mere willing, unless the salvation itself is said to be nothing. Nor again can that desire and endeavor be a mere willing, because desire must strive and aim for something (such as good), and cannot go forth into nothing, nor be absolutely inactive. In a word, wherever the Diatribe turns, it cannot keep clear of inconsistencies and contradictory assertions, nor avoid making that very free will which it defends, as much a prisoner as it is itself. In attempting to free the will it gets so entangled that it ends up bound together with free will in bonds indissoluble!

(Erasmus 14-16, 22-23)
Erasmus' Confusion in Scriptural Proofs

... [673] ... [you are employing] Arguments of Lady Reason . . . Reason, by her conclusions and syllogisms interprets and twists the Scriptures of God whichever way she likes. I shall enter upon this dispute willingly and with confidence, knowing that her babblings are folly and absurdity, especially when she attempts to make a show of her wisdom in divine matters.

First then, I should demand of her how it can be proven that the free will in man is signified and implied wherever the phrase "if thou wilt," "if thou shalt do," "if thou shalt hear" are used. She will say, because the nature of words and the common use of language among men seem to require it. Therefore, she judges of divine things and words according to the customs and things of men. What can be more perverse than that, when the former are heavenly and the latter earthly? Thus like a fool she exposes herself as thinking of God only as of man . . . [677] . . . Wherefore, the words of the law are spoken, not that they might assert the power of the will, but that they might illuminate the blindness of reason. Thus it may seem that its own light is nothing and the power of the will is nothing. "Through law comes the recognition of sin" says Paul (Romans 3,20).

He does not say the abolition or avoidance of sin. The whole nature and design of the law is to give knowledge, and that of nothing else save of sin, and not to discover or communicate any power whatever. This knowledge is not power, nor does it bring power, but it teaches and shows that there is no power here, but great weakness. And what else can the knowledge of sin be, but the knowledge of our weakness and evil? He does not state that through the law comes knowledge of power or of goodness. All the law does, according to Paul's testimony, is to make sin known. It is from this passage that I derive my answer to you: by the words of law man is admonished and taught what he ought to do, and not what he can do . . . [685] . . . God in his own nature and majesty is to be left alone. In this respect we have nothing to do with Him, nor does He wish us to deal with Him. We have to do with Him as far as He is clothed in and delivered to us by His word . . . God Preached deplores the death which He finds in His people, and which He desires to remove from them . . . But God Hidden in majesty neither deplores, nor takes away death, but works life and death and all things; nor is He kept bound to His Word, but has kept Himself free over all things. The Diatribe is deceived by its own ignorance in making no distinction between God Preached and God Hidden, i.e. between the Word of God and God Himself.

. . . [692] . . . The New Testament proper consists of promises and exhortations, just as the Old Testament proper consists of laws and threats. In the New Testament the gospel is preached. This is nothing else than the word that offers the Spirit and grace for the remission of sins, obtained for us by Christ crucified. It is entirely free, given through the mere mercy of God the Father, thus favoring us unworthy creatures who deserve damnation rather than anything else. After this follow exhortations. They are intended to animate those who are already justified and have obtained mercy to be diligent in the fruits of the Spirit and of the righteousness given them, to exercise themselves in love and good works, and to bear courageously the cross and all the other tribulations of this world. This is the whole sum of the New Testament. But how little Erasmus understands of this matter is manifest in not knowing how to distinguish between the Old and the New Testaments. For he sees nothing anywhere but laws and precepts by which men may be formed in good manners. But what the rebirth, renewal, regeneration and the whole work of the Spirit are, he does not see.

. . . [699] . . . And why is it necessary to review one by one all the passages cited from Paul,[23] a collection only of imperative and conditional passages, in which Paul exhorts Christians to the fruits of faith? The Diatribe by its appended conclusion proceeds to envisage a free will whose power is so great that it can do without grace all things Paul prescribes in his exhortations. Christians, however, are not led by a free will, but are driven by the Spirit of God, as Romans 8, 14 tell us. To be driven is not to act or do oneself. But we are so seized as a saw or an ax is handled by a carpenter . . .

. . . Let us consider now the later part where the Diatribe attempts to refute my arguments, i.e., those by which free will is utterly abolished. Here you shall see what the smoke of a man can do against the thunder and lightning of God!

[23] The major portion of this chapter in Luther is a detailed exegetical analysis of many scriptural passages. These have been omitted here.

V

COMMENTS
ON ERASMUS' TREATMENT OF
PASSAGES DENYING FREE WILL*

(Erasmus 30)

Figures of Speech

. . . [700] . . . In this part of the discussion the Diatribe
invents a new trick of eluding the clearest passages, i.e., it
will have it that in the clearest and simplest passages there
is a *trope* (figure of speech). And as before, when speaking
in defense of free will it eluded the force of all the imperative and conditional passages of the law by tacking on
conclusions and similes, so now, where it speaks against me,
it twists all the words of divine promise and declaration,
just as it pleases, by discovering a figure of speech in them
. . . Let this be our sentiment: that no implication or figure
is to be allowed to exist in any passage of Scriptures . . . We
should adhere everywhere to the simple, pure and natural
meaning of the words, according to the rules of grammar
and the habits of speech which God has given unto men . . .
[702] . . . For me this is a serious cause. I want to be as
certain about the truth as I can, in order to settle men's
consciences. I must act very differently. I say then that it
is not enough for you to say there may be a figure. I must

---

* W.A. 699-756

inquire whether there need be and must be a figure. And if you do not prove that there must necessarily be a figure, you achieve nothing . . . The Word of God must be taken in its plain meaning, as the words stand . . .

. . . [703] . . . Let this, therefore, be a fixed and settled point: if the Diatribe cannot prove that there is a figure in these passages which it seeks to overthrow, then it is compelled to grant me that the words must be understood according to their literal meaning, even though it should prove that the same figure is contained in all the other scriptural passages and commonly used by everyone. By gaining this one point, all my arguments which the Diatribe sought to refute are at the same time defended. Thus its refutation is found to achieve nothing.

(Erasmus 31 & 32)

Evil in Man

. . . [709] . . . Perhaps it will be asked how can God be said to work evil in us, in the same way as He is said to harden us, to give us up to our desires, to cause us to err, etc.?

We should indeed be content with the words of God and simply believe what they say, for the works of God are utterly indescribable. However, to humor Reason, i.e., human folly, I will just act the fool and the stupid fellow for once, and try by a little babbling, if I can make any impression upon it . . .

Now then, Satan and man, being fallen and abandoned by God, cannot will good, i.e., things which please God or which God wills, but are ever turned in the direction of their own desires, so that they cannot but seek out their own . . . So that which we call the remnant of nature in Satan and wicked man, as being the creatures and work of God, is no less subject to divine omnipotence and action

than all the rest of the creatures and works of God. Since
God moves and works all in all, He necessarily moves and
works even in Satan and wicked man. But he works according to what they are and what He finds them to be, i.e.,
since they are perverted and evil, being carried along by
that motion of Divine Omnipotence, they cannot but do
what is perverse and evil. Just as it is with a man riding a
horse lame on one foot or on two feet. His riding corre-
sponds to what the horse is. That is, the horse moves badly.
But what can the man do? He is riding this horse together
with sound horses. This one goes badly, though the rest go
well. But it cannot be otherwise, unless the horse be made
sound.

Here you see then that when God works in and by evil
man, evil deeds result. Yet God cannot do evil Himself,
for he is good. He uses evil instruments, which cannot
escape the sway and motion of His Omnipotence. The
fault which accounts for evil being done when God moves
to action lies in these instruments which God does not allow
to lie idle . . . Hence it is that the wicked man cannot but
always err and sin, because under the impulse of divine
power he is not permitted to remain motionless, but must
will, desire and act according to his nature . . . [710] . . .
We are subject to God's working by mere passive necessity
. . . God is incessantly active in all His creatures, allowing
none of them to keep holiday . . . He cannot but do evil by
our evil instrumentality, although He makes good use of
this evil for His own glory and for our salvation. . . . [712]
. . . God is God, for whose will no cause or reason may be
laid down as its rule and measure. For nothing is on a level
with it, not to speak higher. It is itself the measure of all
things. If any rule or measure, or cause or reason existed
for it, it could no longer be the will of God. What God wills
is not right because He ought to or was bound to so will.
On the contrary, what takes place must be right, because
He so wills it.

(Erasmus 33-37)
Foreknowledge and Necessity

. . . [715] Let the Diatribe invent and go on inventing, let it cavil and cavil again, if God foreknew that Judas would be a traitor, Judas became a traitor of necessity, and it was not in the power of Judas, nor of any creature, to alter it, or change his will from that which God had foreseen . . . [716] . . . If God be not deceived in that which he foreknows, then that which He foreknows must of necessity come to pass. Otherwise, who could believe His promises, who would fear His threatenings, if what He promised or threatened did not necessarily ensue? How could He promise or threaten, if His foreknowledge deceives Him or can be hindered by our mutability? This supremely clear light of certain truth manifestly stops all mouths, puts an end to all questions, gives forever victory over all evasive subtleties . . .

. . . [719] . . . Of course, this seems to give the greatest offense to common sense or natural reason, that God, who is proclaimed as being so full of mercy and goodness, should of His own mere will abandon, harden and damn men, as though delighted in the sins and great eternal torments of the miserable. It seems iniquitous, cruel, intolerable to think thus of God. It has given offense to so many and many great men down the ages. And who would not be offended? I myself have been offended at it more than once, even unto the deepest abyss of despair, so far that I wished I had never been made a man. That was before I knew how healthgiving that despair was and how near it was to grace. This is why so much toil and labor has been devoted to excusing the goodness of God, and to accusing the will of man. Here those distinctions have been invented between the ordinary will of God and the absolute will of God, between the necessity of consequence and the necessity of

the thing consequent, and many others. But nothing has
been achieved by these means beyond imposing upon the
unlearned, by vain words and by "the contradictions of
so-called knowledge." [24] For after all, a conscious conviction has been left deeply rooted in the hearts of learned and
unlearned alike, whenever they have made a serious approach to this matter, so that they are aware that, if the
foreknowledge and omnipotence of God are admitted, we
must be under necessity . . .

Luther's Conclusion

[754] What I have to say on this point is as follows:
Man, before he is created to be man does and endeavors
nothing toward his being made a creature. And after he is
made and created, he does and endeavors nothing toward
his preservation as a creature. Both his creation and his
preservation come to pass by the sole will of the omnipotent
power and goodness of God, who creates and preserves us
without ourselves. Yet, God does not work in us without us,
because He created and preserves us for the very purpose
that He might work in us and we might cooperate with
Him, whether that occurs outside His kingdom and under
His general omnipotence, or within His kingdom and under
the special power of His Spirit. So I say that man, before
he is regenerated into the new creation of the Spirit's kingdom does and endeavors nothing to prepare himself, and
when he is regenerated he does and endeavors nothing
toward his perseverance in that kingdom. The Spirit alone,
without ourselves, works both blessings in us, regenerating
us and preserving us when regenerated . . .

. . . [755] . . . I will not accept or tolerate that moderate
middle way which Erasmus would, with good intention, I
think, recommend to me: to allow a certain little to free
will, in order to remove the contradictions of Scripture and

---

[24]   Cf. 1 Timothy 6, 20.

the aforementioned difficulties. The case is not bettered, nor anything gained by this middle way. Because, unless you attribute all and everything to free will, as the Pelagians do, the contradictions in Scripture still remain, merit and reward, the mercy and justice of God are abolished, and all the difficulties which we try to avoid by allowing this certain little ineffective power to free will, remain just as they were before. Therefore, we must go to extremes, deny free will altogether and ascribe everything to God!

VI

SUMMARY
ON THE BONDAGE OF THE WILL *

[756] We are now coming to the last part of this book, in which, as I promised, I am bringing forward my own resources against free will. Not that I shall produce them all, for who could do that within the limits of this small book, when the whole Scriptures, in every letter and iota, stand on my side? There is no need, because free will lies vanquished and prostrate already . . .

Doctrine of Salvation by Faith in Christ Disproves Free Will

. . . [767] . . . Paul now proclaims with full confidence and authority: "But now the righteousness of God has been made manifest independently of the Law, being attested by the Law and the Prophets; the righteousness of God through faith in Jesus Christ upon all who believe. For there is no distinction, as all have sinned and have need of the glory of God. They are justified freely by his grace through the redemption which is in Christ Jesus, whom God has set forth as a propitiation by his blood through faith, etc." (Romans 3,21-25). Here Paul utters very thunderbolts against free will. First, he says, the righteousness of God without the law is manifested. He distinguishes the righteousness of God from the righteousness of the Law, because the righteousness of faith comes by grace, without the law. This saying, "without the law" can mean nothing

---

* W.A. 756-786

else, but that Christian righteousness exists without the works of the law; the works of the law availing and effecting nothing toward its attainment. As [Paul] says further on: "For we reckon that a man is justified by faith independently of the works of the law" (Romans 3,28). And earlier he has said: "For by the works of the law no human being shall be justified" (Romans 3,20). From all this it is clearly manifest that the endeavor and effect of free will are simply nothing. For if the righteousness of God exists without the law, and without the works of the law, how shall it not much more exist without free will? The supreme concern of free will is to exercise itself in moral righteousness, or the works of that law by which its blindness and impotency derive their assistance. But this word "without" abolishes all morally good works, all moral righteousness and all preparations for grace. Scrape together every power you can think of as belonging to free will and Paul will still stand invincible saying, the righteousness of God exists without it! And though I should grant that free will by its endeavors can advance in some direction, namely, unto good works, or unto the righteousness of the civil or moral law, it does yet not advance towards God's righteousness, nor does God in any respect allow its devoted efforts to be worthy unto gaining His righteousness; for He says that His righteousness stands without the law . . .

Personal Comfort in the Doctrine of Bondage

. . . [783] . . . As for myself, I frankly confess, that I should not want free will to be given me, even if it could be, nor anything else be left in my own hands to enable me to strive after my salvation. And that, not merely, because in the face of so many dangers, adversities and onslaughts of devils, I could not stand my ground and hold fast my free will—for one devil is stronger than all men, and on these terms no man could be saved—but because, even though there were no dangers, adversities or devils, I should still be forced to labor with no guarantee of success and to beat the air only. If I lived and worked to all eternity, my conscience would never reach comfortable certainty as to how much it must do to satisfy God. Whatever work it had done, there would still remain a scrupling as to whether or not it pleased God, or whether He required something more. The experience of all who seek righteousness by works proves that. I learned it by bitter experience over a period of many years. But now that God has put my salvation out of the control of my own will and put it under the control of His, and has promised to save me, not according to my effort or running, but . . . according to His own grace and mercy, I rest fully assured that He is faithful and will not lie to me, and that moreover He is great and powerful, so that no devils and no adversities can destroy Him or pluck me out of His hand . . . I am certain that I please God, not by the merit of my works, but by reason of His merciful favor promised to me. So that, if I work too little or badly, He does not impute it to me, but, like a father, pardons me and makes me better. This is the glorying which all the saints have in their God!

VII

CONCLUSION*

[786] I shall here end this book, though prepared, if necessary, to pursue this Discussion still further . . . And now, my friend Erasmus, I entreat you for Christ's sake to keep your promise. You promised that you would willingly yield to him who taught better than yourself . . . I confess that you are a great man, adorned with many of God's noblest gifts, with talent, learning and an almost miraculous eloquence, whereas I have and am nothing, except to glory in being a Christian.

Moreover, I give you hearty praise: alone, in contrast to all others, you have discussed the real thing, i.e., the essential point. You have not wearied me with those irrelevant points about the Papacy, purgatory, indulgences and such trifles . . . For that I heartily thank you . . .

However, if you cannot treat this issue differently from the way this Diatribe does, I pray you, remain content with your own gift and study, adorn and promote literature and the languages, as hitherto you have done to great advantage and with much credit. I confess that your studies have also helped me. For them I honor and sincerely respect you. But God has not willed yet, nor granted you to be equal [to the subject matter of this debate]. [787] I entreat you, do not think me arrogant, when I pray that the Lord may speedily make you as much superior to me in these matters, as you are superior to me in all others. It is nothing new for God to instruct a Moses by a Jethro, or to teach a Paul by an

---

* W.A. 786-787

Ananias. And as to what you say, "you have greatly missed the mark, if you are ignorant of Christ": I think you see yourself how matters stand. But not all will err, if you or I may err. God is glorified in a wonderful way in His saints! So that we may consider those being saints that are farthest from sanctity. Nor is it an unlikely thing that you, as being a man, should fail to understand aright, and to note with sufficient care, the Scriptures, or the sayings of the Fathers, under whose guidance you imagine you cannot miss the mark.

That you have failed is quite clear from this: "you assert nothing, but have made comparisons." One who is fully acquainted with the matter and understands it, does not write like that. On the contrary, in this book of mine, I have not made comparisons, but have asserted and still do assert. I wish none to become judges, but urge all men to submit!

May the Lord whose cause this is, enlighten you and make you a vessel of honor and glory. Amen.